THE UNIVERSITY OF CHICAGO
ORIENTAL INSTITUTE SEMINARS
NUMBER 1

Series Editors
Thomas A. Holland
and
Thomas G. Urban

CHANGING SOCIAL IDENTITY WITH THE SPREAD OF ISLAM
ARCHAEOLOGICAL PERSPECTIVES

edited by

DONALD WHITCOMB

with Case Studies by

JODI MAGNESS, TRACY HOFFMAN,
YURY KAREV, MARK C. HORTON,
and
TIMOTHY INSOLL

THE ORIENTAL INSTITUTE OF THE UNIVERSITY OF CHICAGO
ORIENTAL INSTITUTE SEMINARS • NUMBER 1
CHICAGO • ILLINOIS

Library of Congress Control Number: 2004117327
ISBN: 1-885923-34-1

The Oriental Institute, Chicago

Series Editors' Acknowledgments

The assistance of Katherine Strange Burke, Lindsay
DeCarlo, Katie L. Johnson, Leslie Schramer, Alexandra
Witsell, and Ilya Yakubovich is acknowledged in the pro-
duction of this volume.

Front Cover Illustration

Egypt Gaziret Quoma
Muslim man who has painted his pilgrimage to the
Haj on his home.
©Hutchison Picture Library/Chris Parker

Title Page and Back Cover Illustration

Ballas style of water pot, excavated at Quseir al-
Qadim in Egypt and dated to the fourteenth
century. This pot is in the same tradition as the
Nubian water jar in the front cover illustration and
continues to have a widespread distribution in contemporary Egypt.

Printed by McNaughton & Gunn, Saline, Michigan

TABLE OF CONTENTS

PREFACE

The goal of this seminar was a comparative analysis of different sites and regions, based on archaeological monuments or artifacts, exploring processes of adaptation or adjustment to local cultural complexes. Islamic archaeology in Chicago's Department of Near Eastern Languages and Civilization may claim to be one of the few doctoral programs that stresses archaeology rather than art history. This seminar was the first in a new program initiated by Professor Gil Stein, Director of the Oriental Institute, and we are grateful for his recognition of the potential of this field of studies. The seminars are intended to result in a monograph and we are grateful to Thomas Urban, Oriental Institute Publications Office, for overseeing the production of this volume. A special thanks may also be offered to Ms. Katherine Strange Burke, a doctoral candidate in Islamic Archaeology, for her analysis of the Roundtable discussions, copy editing the papers submitted, and page setting the final proofs. Finally we would thank Ms. Nicole Torres for organizing facilities and hospitality in Chicago.

The participants and their papers were:

- Dr. Tracy Hoffman (University of Chicago), "Ascalon: Domestic Architecture in a Byzantine-Islamic City"

- Prof. Renata Holod (University of Pennsylvania), "Territory and Text: Reconstructing Settlement on Medieval and Early Modern Jerba" (to be published elsewhere)

- Prof. Mark C. Horton (University of Bristol), "Islam, Archaeology, and Swahili Identity"

- Prof. Timothy Insoll (University of Manchester), "Syncretism, Identity, and Islamic Archaeology in West Africa"

- Dr. Yury Karev (Russian Academy of Sciences, Moscow), "Samarqand in VIII Century, the Evidence of Transformation"

- Prof. Jodi Magness (University of North Carolina, Chapel Hill), "Khirbet Abu Suwwana: An Early Islamic Village Near Jerusalem"

Principal discussants at the Roundtable included:

- Dr. Moain Sadeq (Palestinian Department of Antiquities in Gaza), Prof. Fred Donner (University of Chicago), and Dr. John Meloy (American University in Beirut)

LIST OF ABBREVIATIONS

A.H.   *anno Hegirae*, in the year of [Muhammad's] Hegira
C.E.   of the common era
cm   centimeter(s)
diss.   dissertation
e.g.   *exempli gratia*, for example
fig(s).   figure(s)
ha   hectare(s)
ibid.   *ibidem*, in the same place
i.e.   *id est*, that is
km   kilometer(s)
m   meter(s)
p(p).   pages(s)
pl(s).   plate(s)

LIST OF FIGURES

INTRODUCTION

THE SPREAD OF ISLAM AND ISLAMIC ARCHAEOLOGY

DONALD WHITCOMB

The Oriental Institute of the University of Chicago

On the 12th and 13th of May 2003, an unusual group of archaeologists gathered for a seminar in the Oriental Institute of the University of Chicago. This assembly was unusual in that individual specializations varied in geography, from West Africa to Central Asia, and in chronological focus, from the seventh into the sixteenth centuries. The unifying factor was a common concern for the regional impact of the spread of Islam and the process of its adoption within each antecedent culture. One further element was a somewhat unusual attention to archaeological evidence for interpreting social change. The following introduction attempts to suggest the archaeological background for this seminar, then introduce some aspects of the case studies presented here. The comments attempt to give a sense of the Roundtable discussion that allowed the participants to react to each others ideas and look for common patterns on the subject of social change.

The spread of Islam is a historical process that has multifaceted interpretations, rarely neutrally observed either in the seventh century, the thirteenth century, or indeed in the modern world. Explanations of this process and in particular its successes have been attempted by historians and more recently by archaeologists. One important example is the impact of Henri Pirenne's historical theses and the re-analysis by David Whitehouse and Richard Hodges, and again by Hodges.[1] These latter studies have relied on syntheses of widespread sources of archaeological investigations. While the "barrier" of the Mediterranean has been effectively discarded, more subtle conceptual constraints of core and periphery, urbanized and undeveloped, regionalism, ethnic characterization, and so forth, tend to limit broader understandings. New approaches to all these aspects are major concerns in modern archaeological research.

This seminar recalls a rather different conference of fifty years ago, organized by anthropologists and Islamicists from Chicago but held in Germany.[2] This meeting was one of a series of "Comparative Studies in Cultures and Civilizations" organized by Robert Redfield in order to compare research in different countries toward a common understanding of cultural patterns. The conference organized by Gustave E. von Grunebaum may seem today heavily philological and perhaps even "orientalist" in emphasis. This in turn recalls another conference, this time in London during 1972, which presented a series of comparative studies on "conversion to Islam." This conference was quite innocent of archaeology, though its convener, Nehemia Levtzion, mentions the need for imagination and new methods and immediately suggests the important po-

---

1. R. Hodges and D. Whitehouse, *Mohammed, Charlemagne and the Origins of Europe: Archaeology and the Pirenne Thesis* (London, 1983). See also, R. Hodges, *Towns and Trade in the Age of Charlemagne* (London, 2000).

2. Gustave E. von Grunebaum, "Islamic Studies and Cultural Research," in *Studies in Islamic Cultural History*, edited by Gustave E. von Grunebaum (American Anthropological Association, Memoir 76; Menasha, 1954), pp. 1–22.

tential for archaeological evidence.[3] Islamic archaeology has a long tradition of contributions to art historical studies of the Middle East, as noted below. The wider utilization for Islamic history is only recently coming to the fore; one might note that none of the archaeological evidence reported in this volume was available until after the early 1970s. These studies bring innovative approaches to Islam and the Islamic tradition, beyond the pioneering efforts to understand historical phenomena through archaeology. A continuing strategy is the juxtaposition of different fields of study to realize common patterns of information and interpretation.

THE ROLE OF ISLAMIC ARCHAEOLOGY

Islamic archaeology has been practiced for about a century, and more importantly, significant growth has taken place in this field in recent times. The earliest excavation in each new region was usually a high-profile, large site of symbolic importance. Samarra remains the archetype with an underlying purpose of aesthetically significant discoveries; yet even this site has found significant reinterpretations (alas, without further excavations).[4] The next stage in the development of Islamic archaeology was the multiplication of investigations of specialized sites; more than common tells, citadels, ports, and especially "desert castles" were examined as classes of comparable examples. An archaeological alternative to this approach was the regional survey resulting from the contextualization of elements into a broadly functional logic. The next stage for Islamic archaeology is a focus on socio-cultural or historical problem solving.

While an indirect relation to archaeological programs is implied in other periods, the professionalization of the discipline of Islamic archaeology requires a formal consideration of methodology. Treatment of artifacts using a distinctively archaeological methodology begins with the unique context of assemblages of abstracted types and employs a comparative mode of analysis to produce patterns of data sets. Such archaeological patterns are internally generated but do not usually exist outside of an interpretative framework, the socio-historical matrix. Thus archaeological procedures are distinctive and capable of producing information and understanding inaccessible by other modes of analysis. Archaeology is not any study of old or excavated artifacts, it is a specific procedure with the goal of producing generalizing interpretations on various scales of abstraction.

Alternative archaeologies may be defined as a search for new contexts.[5] Thus for Timothy Insoll, definition of this field is found in the explicit archaeology of religion, and he attempts to make the case that material culture may be seen consistently through cultic or spiritual influences of this alternative archaeology.[6] Islamic archaeology is practiced as a historical archaeology providing vital evidence for the development of society and economy in Islamic

3. Nehemia Levtzion, "Toward a Comparative Study of Islamization," in *Conversion to Islam*, edited by Nehemia Levtzion (New York, 1979), p. 4. Levtzion specifically mentions the inscriptions published by J. Sauvaget, "Les épitaphes royales de Gao," *Bulletin de l'Institut fondamental d'Afrique noire* 12 (1950): 318–40.

4. See C. F. Robinson, editor, *A Medieval Islamic City Reconsidered: An Interdisciplinary Approach to Samarra* (Oxford, 2001).

5. Or put somewhat better, "From a methodological point of view, much of the theoretical debate in today's archaeology can be seen as a search for new contexts" (A. Andrén, *Between Artifacts and Texts: Historical Archaeology in Global Perspective* [New York, 1998], p. 155).

6. Timothy Insoll, *The Archaeology of Islam* (Oxford, 1999). Insoll's approach to archaeology has its roots in the University of Cambridge school of post-processual theoretical endeavors; the field of archaeology of religion is one of these branches. See also Donald Whitcomb, "Review of *The Archaeology of Islam*, by Timothy Insoll," *American Journal of Archaeology* 104 (2000): 413–14.

contexts. Each project, whatever its intended goals, produces informative associations that may be applied to relevant textual sources.

The intention of this seminar was not reduction to a sort of essentialism but regional comparisons exploring Islamic archaeology from different disciplinary perspectives. The comparative analysis of different sites and regions, based on archaeological monuments or artifacts, allows an exploration of processes of adaptation or adjustment to local cultural complexes. Islam may be seen as a religion, political system, and cultural complex, a trinity of inseparable aspects. The introduction of these variable characteristics of Islam, during its contact with an antecedent culture and afterwards, resulted in changes in identity approached as a sort of "cognitive" archaeology. In each specific case, one may assess the nature of the pre-Islamic regional tradition, the resulting plurality of cultures as a "multi-cultural" society, and finally a resultant normative condition as a regional or cosmopolitan culture.

THE SPREAD OF ISLAM

The Islamicization of the Middle East (and beyond) has its origins in the Muslim conquest of the early seventh century. Explanations of this conquest seem to fail modern scholars no less than the Byzantines and Sasanians who actually confronted this movement. Fred M. Donner's extensive analysis moves away from dissatisfactory militaristic explanations toward changes in "social organization."[7] While the initial successes of Islam became a state acquisition of territory, the later and long-term adherence to Islam may be sought in social interactions which resulted in a shift of identity. As Nehemia Levtzion notes, "Islamization of a social or ethnic group is not a single act of conversion but a long process toward greater conformity and orthodoxy."[8] Conformity (and orthodoxy) may find expression in the adoption of architecture and objects as signs and ultimately symbols of this new identity. Thus variations repeated in vastly different regions and times may form patterns not completely explained through textual resources but amenable to archaeological analysis. The purpose of this seminar was to adduce a very limited number of specific examples toward this patterning in the spread of Islam.

The early period presents a dual problem during the establishment of political control over pre-existing cultures: first, the self-formulation of Islamic society; and second, formulation of a multi-cultural society. The resulting configuration is defined as Islamic, both politically and culturally. In later periods, complexities of Islamic cultures lead to varied experiences of expansion and domination. Philip L. Kohl's Islamic archaeology is an archaeology without Islam, a medieval and pre-modern archaeology of the Middle East.[9] This approach stands in direct contrast to that of Insoll, whose view of Islam is essentially non-historical and tends to offer a static description of Islamic religion.[10] The following case studies are not a search for answers but examples drawn from archaeological evidence to be utilized with historical information for more sophisticated narratives and perhaps models and theories of development.

---

7. Fred M. Donner, *The Early Islamic Conquests* (Princeton, 1981), p. 269; an understanding of these changes in consideration of the character of historical sources is expanded in Fred M. Donner, *Narratives of Islamic Origins: The Beginnings of Islamic Historical Writing* (Princeton, 1998).

8. Nehemia Levtzion, "Toward a Comparative Study of Islamization," p. 21.

9. Philip L. Kohl, "The Material Culture of the Modern Era in the Ancient Orient: Suggestions for Future Work," *Domination and Resistance*, edited by D. Miller, M. Rowlands, and C. Tilly (London, 1989), pp. 240–45; he discusses Islamic archaeology from an "evolutionary focus," as a backdrop for Western capitalism and colonialism.

10. Insoll, *Archaeology of Islam*, p. 13.

THE CASE STUDIES

We begin with Abu Suwwana in one of the most intensively studied regions, through both regional surveys and excavations. There is modern revisionism: on one side Neil A. Silberman, in his "thundering hoards," exposes the fixed models and agenda inherited from Biblical archaeology;[11] on the other hand, Yehuda Nevo attempts to apply the current debate on the nature of early Islamic historical sources to archaeological evidence (producing new, agenda-driven distortions).[12] Located on the desert periphery, Abu Suwwana was a rescue excavation of an early Islamic site, recovering the mosque and residences of a large village. The sophisticated debate on chronology is possible through the detailed publication of all artifacts, typical of modern archaeology in Israel. The study of ceramics has advanced significantly with the research of Jodi Magness, Miriam Avissar, and Ya'el Arnon, all based on controlled excavations of Islamic sites. Ein 'Aneva, though an isolated building, is offered as a comparandum for chronology and rural architecture. The original implication that the site was abandoned (destroyed) by the "thundering" Muslim conquest is effectively countered.

Perhaps the most interesting and valuable contribution in this study is the exposition of modular architecture, a repetition of small parallel rooms. This derives from Mordechai Haiman's depiction of "nucleus units" in the Negev during the early Islamic period and, both agree, reflects a specific social organization, which differs from that implied by dwellings of the Roman and Byzantine periods in Palestine. The Bedouin may become described as undergoing a process of sedentarization from transhumance in Arabia; a very similar pattern was explored in detail at the site of al-Risha by Svend Helms.[13] The result is mixed architecture of modular settlements on the desert periphery in the early Islamic period.[14] These villages are suggestive of the urban changes as a sort of "Polis to Madina" revisited,[15] social and legal explanations repeated, such as the nature of commercialization. These are aspects further explored in the next paper.

Ascalon (or Asqalon) represents archaeology in an urban setting. As Tracy Hoffman points out, the normal indications of change, public institutions such as the mosque, are not available except through limited textual descriptions.[16] Rather, residential structures form the primary evidence of change. There is a continuity in basic structures with some reorganization of interiors,

11. Neil A. Silberman, "Thundering Hordes: The Image of the Persian and Muslim Conquests in Palestinian Archaeology," in *Studies in the Archaeology of Israel and Neighboring Lands in Memory of Douglas L. Esse*, edited by Samuel R. Wolff (Studies in Ancient Oriental Civilization 59; American Schools of Oriental Research Books 5; Chicago and Atlanta, 2001), pp. 611–23. Silberman advocates "a more complex conception of cultural reorganization," largely through archaeological research (ibid., p. 616) and, in context of Magness' paper, a more sophisticated understanding of pastoralists in pre-Islamic as well as Islamic society.

12. This discussion is under the title of "revisionism in the desert" in Donald Whitcomb, "Islam and the Socio-cultural Transition of Palestine, Early Islamic Period (638–1099 C.E.)," in *The Archaeology of Society in the Holy Land*, edited by T. Levy (London, 1995), pp. 488–501.

13. Svend Helms, *Early Islamic Architecture of the Desert: A Bedouin Station in Eastern Jordan* (Edinburgh, 1990).

14. Whether this locational characteristic is selective or accident of preservation remains to be explored.

15. This refers to the seminal article by H. Kennedy, "From Polis to Madina: Urban Change in Late Antique and Early Islamic Syria," *Past and Present* 106 (1985): 3–27. One also finds echoes of an "appropriation of the land," suggested by O. Grabar, *The Formation of Islamic Art* (New Haven, 1973).

16. This paper is abstracted from her dissertation, successfully defended shortly before this conference, Tracy Hoffman, "Ascalon 'Arus ash-Sham: The Archaeology and History of a Byzantine–Early Islamic City" (Ph.D. diss., University of Chicago, 2003).

as well as suggestions of neighborhood changes. By intriguing coincidence the urban code of Julian of Ascalon makes clear that urban changes began well before the advent of Islam. Fustat houses are used to illustrate how this structural pattern continues in the prototypical "Islamic city." The resulting picture is an urban phenomenon which builds, as one might expect, from pre-Islamic forms but in a new organizational pattern, a model that may be tested on other Middle Eastern cities. Most importantly, one has a pattern that avoids the assumptions and dictations of studies of European cities. This new type of medieval city may be seen as determined by physical, formal attributes, moving beyond the subjective "feel" of the Islamic city, which Doris Behrens-Abouseif so beautifully describes.[17]

At the same time that Arabs were settling into Palestinian villages and perhaps rehabilitating the old houses of Ascalon, their armies set out from the *amsar* (Islamic urban foundations) in Iraq in large numbers for Central Asia. They proceeded to colonize and rule these ancient lands of the East. Samarqand was a capital of the Soghdian rulers, a distinct region located between the Chinese and Sasanian empires. Yury Karev describes the archaeological evidence for the development of this frontier of the first Muslim empire. His account is based on his participation in French-Russian projects at Afrasiab, the site of medieval (and ancient) Samarqand. Despite, or possibly because of, the exotic location of Samarqand, this project may represent a more traditional archaeology, large-scale clearance of major architectural monuments on the citadel and "sacred area." This is a careful analysis of fragmentary historical documentation balanced with stratigraphic and architectural analyses, which are perhaps even more fragmentary and challenging, toward the goal of reconstruction of a historical narration of urban development.

As one might expect, Soghdian antecedents are mixed with architecture and artifacts typical of the western parts of the Muslim empire (e.g., Amman citadel). The view from the citadel is one emphasizing the political change and implied acceptance by the elites, an aspect particular to the conquest period and in line with the "official view" found in documentary sources. At Marv, there are reports of massive Arab settlement in the villages, which may present another side of this process.[18] There is a need to look at regional archaeological evidence with Samarqand as a part of a larger pattern, a perspective forced on archaeologists dealing with archaeology in sub-Saharan Africa.

Mark C. Horton's comprehensive presentation of Swahili culture provides an introduction to a peripheral region of some archaeological vitality.[19] The history of its archaeology is colonial in two senses: the political milieu of its first practitioners and the dominant model for Swahili culture, which led to an archaeology with "a very oriental interpretation [focusing] on stone towns and their architecture," thought to be importations of Arab and Persian culture. Horton touches upon current revisionism stressing the dominance and continuity of the Tana tradition, early Iron Age cultural patterns of the interior of East Africa. This debate has a correlate in the material evidence of Islamic culture explored by Michael G. Morony;[20] this approach often pre-

---

17. Doris Behrens-Abouseif, "La conception de la ville dans la pensée arabe du Moyen Âge," in *Mégapoles méditerranéennes: Géographie urbaine rétrospective*, edited by C. Nicolet (Paris, 2000), pp. 32–40.

18. Paul Wheatley, *The Places Where Men Pray Together: Cities in Islamic Lands, Seventh through the Tenth Centuries* (Chicago, 2001), pp. 187–89, on Samarqand, see pp. 312–14.

19. One may note a recent synthesis of archaeological research in East Africa; S. Pradines, *Fortifications et urbanisation en Afrique orientale* (British Archaeological Reports, International Series 1216; Oxford, 2004).

20. Donald Whitcomb, "Toward a 'Common Denominator': An Archaeological Response to M. Morony on Pottery and Urban Identities," in *Identity and Material Culture in the Early Islamic World*, edited by I. Bierman (Los Angeles, 1995), pp. 47–68.

sents a dichotomy between regional traditions and cosmopolitan identifications (perhaps an example of the Great Tradition).

Departing from this archaeological tradition of African culture and testing these hypotheses on the role of Islam, Horton analyzes his excavations at Shanga, a large town of the fourteenth century with a central mosque having antecedents going back into the eighth century. He presents the complications deriving from his interpretation of the archaeological evidence, on the nature of buildings, the role in the community, and implications for the arrival and spread of Islam. One fascinating aspect is the utilization of "the Swahili's own oral traditions and chronicles," and in fact, the ethno-historical considerations of a continuing cultural tradition. He contrasts this approach to a more abstracted model of conversion presented by Insoll.[21]

Both scholars are aware of the openings into enlarged debate brought by archaeological research on the role of Islam. Evidence is revealing, such as the large post marking the *miḥrāb*, which has correlates in early mosques of the Middle East. More vexatious is the search for evidence of sectarianism in this Islamic archaeology. Horton uses the example of Ibadism as a search for evidence of imported rites; this led to a lively discussion in the Roundtable session on the comparative Ibadi evidence from the island of Jerba.[22]

Insoll takes the problem of Islamization directly across the continent of Africa to the Gao region of Mali. He uses this example for a phased conversion model that views the process as one of syncretism, though he recognizes the negative connotations of this term. While he sees conversion as dependent on social grouping, he might have dissected the phases as processes of imitation-hybridization-syncretism methodology in analysis of cultural change.[23] He claims the first to convert are nomad groups. This presents a double irony in that early Islamic tradition questioned the faith or faithfulness of these tribal groups, and of course their evidence is possibly the most difficult to detect archaeologically.

Not surprisingly, Insoll concentrates on urban elements, though his fluidity in population composition may be overstated or peculiar to West Africa. Unlike his earlier account of this process, he has left out the crucial stage of conversion of ruler (and associated elites) that is found in so many other instances. Urban complexes are the location of most archaeological evidence, while the *pagani* of rural localities are seen, not surprisingly, as the most conservative. His last group to convert brings us back to rural Palestine and the evidence of early Muslim communities there. Again his discussion of residual "cults" may find reference in Nevo's misguided revisionism (as noted above). One might ask whether the human representations at Jeme-Jenno are so different from the impulse that led to the frescoes adorning Qusayr 'Amra in Jordan.

Thus, Insoll's hypotheses inspire comparative observations and may spark a reconsideration of implications from the material evidence from the previous case studies. As with the other papers presented here, there is a patterning through contextualizations, which is shown to be the fundamental methodology of archaeology. He ends with a note on the "privilege of archaeolo-

---

21. This is found in his detailed survey, Timothy Insoll, "The Archaeology of Islam in Sub-Saharan Africa: A Review," *Journal of World Prehistory* 10 (1996): 439–504, and Timothy Insoll, *The Archaeology of Islam in Sub-Saharan Africa* (Cambridge, 2003).

22. Renata Holod, "The Medieval and Early Modern Periods on Jerba: A Preliminary Report on the Jerba Archaeological Survey," *Africa* (forthcoming). It is particularly to be regretted that her paper at this seminar, "Territory and Text: Reconstructing Settlement on Medieval and Early Modern Jerba," could not be included here. On North Africa, one may consult P. Pentz, *From Roman Proconsularis to Islamic Ifriqiyah* (Göteborg, 2002).

23. Tasha Vorderstrasse, "A Port of Antioch under Byzantium, Islam, and the Crusades: Acculturation and Differentiation at al-Mina, A.D. 350–1268" (Ph.D. diss., University of Chicago, 2004).

gists" to have access to information on these processes of change. In an earlier study, he emphasizes "the privileged position of the Islamic archaeologist as an observer of a living religion." This activity is indeed privileged but is usually labeled ethnography; historical archaeology has important implications for present populations, as explored in great detail by Silberman.[24]

CONCLUSIONS

Finally one may note that discussion at the Roundtable turned around two concerns: the nature of questions asked of archaeological data and the relationship of this data to documentary resources. For instance, some would suggest that the first century be treated as "prehistoric" since documentation is so unreliable. Others would counter that interpretation of texts is always important, but this is a critical operation just as is the interpretation of artifacts by archaeologists. Studies of identity, a prominent concern in modern archaeology, adhere to varied fields of theory and continue to struggle with the use of textual documentation or ethnological analogies.[25] Islamic archaeology needs to establish methodologies comparable to other branches of modern archaeological study that provide frameworks for structuring material evidence and the resultant historical narratives. One approach is to begin with the example of Muqaddasi, a tenth century scholar who stressed geographical organization, not unlike the regional structure of the seminar.[26]

Exposure to unfamiliar subjects and historical perspectives were not sufficient to initiate abstract comparative modeling in a couple of days, though this may be hoped for in the future.

24. Timothy Insoll, *The Archaeology of Islam*, p. 54. See Neil A. Silberman, *Between Past and Present: Archaeology, Ideology, and Nationalism in the Modern Middle East* (New York, 1989).

25. S. Shennan, editor, *Archaeological Approaches to Cultural Identity* (London, 1989).

26. One may agree that "Geographical evidence has a clear advantage over historical information in that it is not so susceptible to dispute" (M. Lecker, *Muslims, Jews and Pagans: Studies on Early Islamic Medina* [Leiden, 1995]), p. 147.

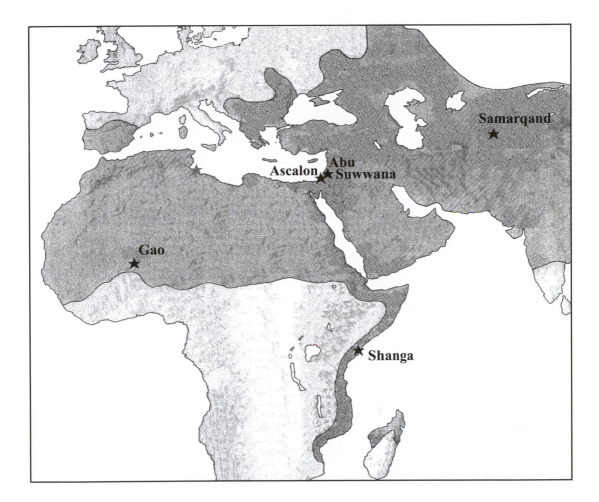

Figure 1. The spread of Islam and selected archaeological sites
(adapted from D. Nicolle, *Historical Atlas of the Islamic World* [New York, 2003], pp. 6–7)

1

KHIRBET ABU SUWWANA AND EIN ʿANEVA: TWO EARLY ISLAMIC SETTLEMENTS ON PALESTINE'S DESERT PERIPHERY

JODI MAGNESS

University of North Carolina at Chapel Hill

The history and archaeology of Palestine's early Islamic cities and towns such as Jerusalem, Ramla, Tiberias, and Caesarea are relatively well known. However, small villages and farm-steads, especially in remote rural regions, have attracted less scholarly attention. In this paper, I consider two early Islamic settlements located on Palestine's desert periphery: Khirbet Abu Suwwana and Ein ʿAneva (see fig. 2.1 in Hoffman article). First, I examine and correct the chronology of each settlement and suggest that they date to the eighth to ninth centuries. I then consider the information that the layout of these settlements provides for changes in the social structure of some Palestinian villages during the early Islamic period.

KHIRBET ABU SUWWANA

Khirbet Abu Suwwana is the site of an early Islamic village located near Maʿaleh Adumim, to the east of Jerusalem. In 1991, Ofer Sion conducted a rescue excavation at the site.[1] The excavation in three areas on the west (A, B, C) revealed a crowded system of residential units and a mosque (see fig. 1.1), while in Area D to the east six residential units of high quality were uncovered. Here I focus on the first of two main occupation periods that were distinguished. This period, to which most of the ceramic finds and five of the six coins belong, showed evidence of two sub-phases, which were dated by Sion as follows: Phase 1, from the second half of the seventh century to the first half of the eighth century (the Umayyad period); during this period most of the settlement was founded and reached its peak; Phase 2, from the second half of the eighth century to the first half of the ninth century; during this period the settlement declined. The second main period, after an occupation gap of 300 years, is dated to the Crusader period and is characterized by nomadic settlement in the structures.[2]

The mosque is located on the northern side of Area A, among the twenty-two rooms and courtyards that made up this residence. It had a doorway in the north wall, with a *miḥrāb* opposite. Sion estimated that the mosque could have accommodated up to fifty-four worshipers (in three rows of eighteen each).[3] Except for the mosque, the rooms at the site were not plastered. The stone walls were laid directly on exposed bedrock, following the topography. Most of the

---

1. See Ofer Sion, "Khirbet Abu Suwwana," ʿAtiqot 32 (1997): 183–94 (in Hebrew with English summary on p. 50*; the pottery is published separately in English by Joelle Cohen Finkelstein, "The Islamic Pottery from Khirbet Abu Suwwana," ʿAtiqot 32 [1997]: 19*–34*). A preliminary report on the ex-

cavations was published by Ofer Sion, "Khirbet Abu Suwwana," Excavations and Surveys in Israel 13 (1995): 66–67.
2. Sion, "Khirbet Abu Suwwana," p. 50*.
3. Sion, "Khirbet Abu Suwwana," p. 184.

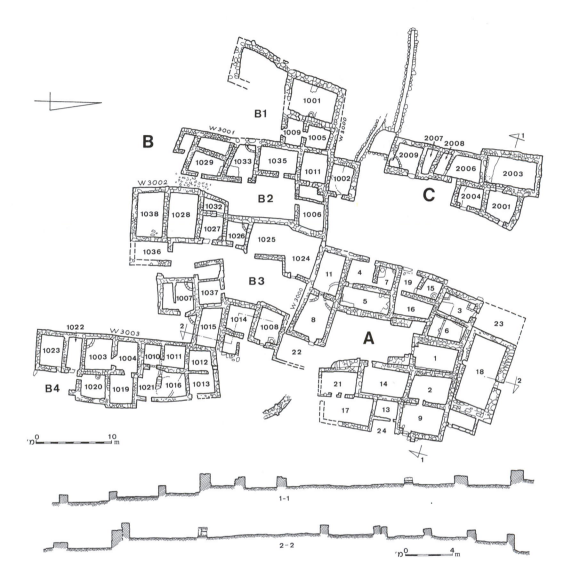

Figure 1.1. Plan of Areas A, B, and C at Khirbet Abu Suwwana (from Ofer Sion, "Khirbet Abu Suwwana," *ʿAtiqot* 32 [1997]: fig. 3; reprinted with permission of the Israel Antiquities Authority)

floors were of packed dirt and lime, and with one exception, all of the roofs were apparently flat and of wood. The dwellings consisted of courtyards and spacious rooms, with numerous ovens and installations.[4] Most of the few bones recovered were identified as sheep and chickens, from floor levels and near ovens. An infant burial found below the floor in Unit D6, about 0.5 m below floor level is probably Bedouin.[5]

Sion estimated the population of the settlement during Phase 1 at about two hundred inhabitants, based on the assumption that five people lived in each room, and the calculation that 40% of the 100 rooms excavated were used for dwelling purposes. The presence of agricultural installations and pens indicates that the economy was based on agriculture and animal husbandry. Many pens were surveyed inside and outside the village; more than ten are scattered at a distance of up to 250 m from the site. Smaller pens are located within the village. If each herd had sixty to eighty sheep, the total estimated number of sheep was 600–800. No other early Islamic sites were found in surveys to the east of the site, but seven were identified in surveys to the north, and twelve more to the south. Only three others were of the same size as Khirbet Abu Suwwana. During Phase 2, the settlement at Khirbet Abu Suwwana declined, and the population decreased by 35%.[6]

Sion's chronology and historical conclusions are based on the numismatic and ceramic evidence. Eight coins were found at the site: one of Anastasius I (498–518); three Umayyad coins (one of 700–749; a fragment dating to before 749; and a third that is post-reform, of 697–749); one Umayyad or ʿAbbasid coin (about 750); a Byzantine-Arab coin; a Crusader coin; and one unidentified coin, perhaps of the eighth or ninth century.[7] 85% of the ceramic material and five out of six of the coins belong to the first main occupation period, mostly to Phase 1. 87% of the finds from the rooms in Area A are from the seventh to eighth centuries. According to Sion, most of the ceramic material from the mosque and the bronze coin (no. 2, Umayyad, 700–749, from the floor level in Room 18) indicate that the mosque was constructed in the second half of the seventh century, while the rest of the finds, which are from Phase 2, date from the eighth to ninth centuries. Soundings dug to bedrock in most of the rooms in Areas B and C revealed just one occupation level.[8] The floors in L1003 and 1026 (Area B) and L1027 (Area C) were dated on the basis of the ceramic material from the seventh to eighth centuries. According to Sion, Unit B2 was continuously occupied until the ninth century, whereas Rooms 1007, 1008, 1010, 1017, 1024, 1026, and 1038 were neglected/abandoned during Phase 2. All of the rooms in Area C were built during Phase 1; during Phase 2 Rooms 2001 and 2004 went out of use. Thus, most of the pottery from Area C belongs to Phase 1. Similarly, 67% of the pottery from Area D belongs to Phase 1, and 22% to Phase 2.

Joelle Cohen Finkelstein, who published the pottery from Khirbet Abu Suwwana, noted the absence of signs of destruction that could account for the end of occupation at the site. Few complete or almost complete vessels were found in the excavations, and most of the pottery studied came from fills. Floors were exposed in some of the loci. Usually, only one floor level was con-

---

4. Sion, "Khirbet Abu Suwwana," pp. 183–84.

5. Sion, "Khirbet Abu Suwwana," p. 50*.

6. Sion, "Khirbet Abu Suwwana," p. 192. Sion dated the second sub-phase of the first main occupation period to the ʿAbbasid period and attributed the decline at this time to the tribal revolts in 744–745.

7. Sion, "Khirbet Abu Suwwana," p. 50*, 191; the coins were identified by Rachel Milstein, Gabriela Bijovsky, and Ofer Sion.

8. Sion, "Khirbet Abu Suwwana," p. 191.

structed above bedrock, and sometimes reused. In a few loci an earlier floor level was reached. Limited soundings or full-scale excavations were undertaken below some of the floors in order to reach bedrock. However, since in most cases the material from the floor was not separated from that of the layer between the bedrock and the makeup of the floor, the pottery cannot accurately date the construction of the floors.[9] Finkelstein dated Phase 1 from the mid-seventh century to mid-eighth century, and Phase 2 from the late eighth to early ninth centuries. A review of the ceramic material indicates that this chronology is too high. This is most easily demonstrated by examining the pottery from Phase 2, which is when glazed pottery first appears.

Phase 2: The glazed bowls from Phase 2 are made of the well-levigated, sandy buff to pink ware and have the slightly curved walls and flaring rim characteristic of early Islamic glazed bowls.[10] The bowls also have the white slip characteristic of Miriam Avissar's "Fine Glazed Bowls," while their exterior glaze is a feature of that same class.[11] The splashed monochrome green and polychrome glazed decoration on the interiors of many of the bowls corresponds with Avissar's "Fine Glazed Bowls, Types 6–9."[12] The sgrafitto bowls also belong to this class.[13] These early Islamic glazed wares are dated by Avissar to the ninth to tenth centuries, though sgrafitto bowls did not appear before the end of the ninth century.[14] The fact that sgraffito bowls are the least common type at Khirbet Abu Suwwana[15] suggests that Phase 2 should be dated from the ninth century to the first half of the tenth century. This chronology is supported by the other ceramic types found in this phase, which include an incurved rim basin of eighth to tenth century date,[16] buff ware ("Mefjer ware") jugs,[17] early 'Abbasid Mahesh ware vessels,[18] and channel-nozzle oil lamps of the eighth to tenth centuries.[19] The only cooking vessel illustrated from this phase is a neckless, globular pot that has a rim with a lid device, horizontal handles, and no traces of glaze.[20]

9. Finkelstein, "Islamic Pottery," p. 19*.
10. Finkelstein, "Islamic Pottery," 24*, fig. 3:1–2, 4–11 (the bowl in fig. 3:2 has a different profile); idem, "Islamic Pottery," p. 31*; see Miriam Avissar, "The Medieval Pottery," in *Yoqne'am 1: The Late Periods*, edited by Amnon Ben-Tor, Miriam Avissar, and Yuval Portugali (Qedem Reports 3; Jerusalem, 1996), pp. 75, 78. Some have the thicker walls characteristic of Avissar's "Common Glazed Bowls" (Finkelstein, "Islamic Pottery," fig. 3:4–7; Avissar, "The Medieval Pottery," p. 75), while others have the thinner walls seen in her "Fine Glazed Bowls" (Finkelstein, "Islamic Pottery," fig. 3:1, 8, Avissar, "The Medieval Pottery," p. 78). Similarly, both the disc bases characteristic of Avissar's "Common Glazed Bowls" are represented (Finkelstein, "Islamic Pottery," fig. 3:9, 11), and the low ring bases of her "Fine Glazed Bowls" (Finkelstein, "Islamic Pottery," fig. 3:10; Avissar, "The Medieval Pottery," p. 78).
11. Finkelstein, "Islamic Pottery," p. 24*; see Avissar, "The Medieval Pottery," p. 78.
12. Finkelstein, "Islamic Pottery," p. 24*, fig. 3:1–2, 4–7, 9, 11; see Avissar, "The Medieval Pottery," pp. 78–82.
13. Finkelstein, "Islamic Pottery," p. 31*, 24*, Group D, fig. 3:8, 11; see Avissar, "The Medieval Pottery," pp. 81–82, Type 7, "Polychrome Splashed and Mottled Sgrafitto Ware."
14. Avissar, "The Medieval Pottery," pp. 78–82.
15. Finkelstein, "Islamic Pottery," p. 31*.
16. Finkelstein, "Islamic Pottery," p. 22*, fig. 2:1; see Jodi Magness, *Jerusalem Ceramic Chronology, circa 200–800 C.E.* (Sheffield, 1993), pp. 210–11.
17. Finkelstein, "Islamic Pottery," p. 28*, fig. 7:5–6, 8–13; see Avissar, "The Medieval Pottery," pp. 155–61, Types 2–12; James A. Sauer and Jodi Magness, "Ceramics of the Islamic Period," in *The Oxford Encyclopedia of Archaeology in the Near East*, Volume 1, edited by Eric M. Meyers (New York, 1997), pp. 477–78.
18. Finkelstein, "Islamic Pottery," p. 27*, fig. 6:6, 8; 28*, fig. 7:1–4; see Donald Whitcomb, "Mahesh Ware: Evidence of Early Abbasid Occupation from Southern Jordan," *Annual of the Department of Antiquities of Jordan* 33 (1989): 269–85.
19. Finkelstein, "Islamic Pottery," p. 30*, fig. 8; see Magness, *Jerusalem Ceramic Chronology*, pp. 258–59, Oil Lamps Form 5.
20. Finkelstein, "Islamic Pottery," p. 28*, fig. 7:17; see Avissar, "The Medieval Pottery," pp. 132–34; it most closely resembles her Cooking Pots from the Early Islamic Period, Type 1, which differs in having strap handles.

Phase 1: If Phase 2 at Khirbet Abu Suwwana dates from the ninth century to the first half of the tenth century, what is the date of Phase 1? The diagnostic types from Phase 1 include bowls with a mid-seventh to ninth or tenth century range,[21] incurved rim basins,[22] a buff ware bowl,[23] and jars and jugs of buff ware ("Mefjer ware").[24] A metallic buff jug with painted white bands on the shoulder is a type that appeared at Pella in the late sixth century and is represented in the 746/747 destruction level at that site.[25] The storage jars with swollen necks are dated from the late seventh to ninth or tenth centuries.[26] Another type of storage jar characterized by a sharp ridge in the middle of the neck should be assigned to the eighth to ninth centuries.[27] The cooking vessels from Phase 1 include a casserole with horizontal handles, the deep form and dark brown ware of which point to a late seventh/early eighth to ninth or tenth century date.[28] Another cooking pot with globular body, no neck, and two horizontal handles has parallels of tenth to early eleventh century date from Yoqneʿam.[29]

Though some of the ceramic types from Phase 1 have a range beginning in the late sixth to seventh century, the complete absence of types characteristic of Jerusalem in the mid-sixth to late seventh centuries (such as Late Roman red wares, Fine Byzantine Wares of mid-sixth to late seventh century date, and large candlestick oil lamps) provides a late seventh century *terminus post quem* for the establishment of the settlement at Khirbet Abu Suwwana. The ceramic and numismatic evidence thus indicates an eighth century date for Phase 1 and a ninth to early or mid-tenth century date for Phase 2.

EIN ʿANEVA[30]

Ein ʿAneva is a small spring on the south bank of Nahal Zeelim (Wadi Seiyal), about 4 km north of Masada. The spring's output was greater in antiquity than today, and evidence indicates that the water was used to irrigate about ten dunams of agricultural terraces below it and to the west. In the past, a small building to the west of the spring was identified as a Roman fort erected to guard the spring during the siege of Masada in 72/73 C.E.

In 1981 Yosef Porath excavated this structure, which turned out to be a small rectangular dwelling (ca. 6.0×15.5 m) with two similar habitation units aligned on the same axis (see fig. 1.2). This axis was oriented north–south, so that the building was aligned with the riverbed.

21. Finkelstein, "Islamic Pottery," p. 21*, fig. 1:2; 22*, fig. 2:3, 6, 14; Magness, *Jerusalem Ceramic Chronology*, pp. 198–99, Fine Byzantine Ware Bowls Forms 2A and 2B.

22. Finkelstein, "Islamic Pottery," p. 21*, fig. 1:7, 10, fired buff, not dark brown.

23. Finkelstein, "Islamic Pottery," p. 22*, fig. 2:16, Mahesh ware?

24. Finkelstein, "Islamic Pottery," p. 25*, fig. 4:1, 3, 10–11, though not identified as such by Finkelstein.

25. Finkelstein, "Islamic Pottery," p. 25*, fig. 4:6; see Alan G. Walmsley, "The Umayyad Pottery and Its Antecedents," in *Pella in Jordan*, Volume 1: *An Interim Report on the Joint University of Sydney and the College of Wooster Excavations at Pella 1979–1981* (Canberra, 1982), pp. 146–47, 156.

26. Finkelstein, "Islamic Pottery," p. 26*, fig. 5:3–5; Magness, *Jerusalem Ceramic Chronology*, pp. 230–31, Storage Jars Form 7.

27. Finkelstein, "Islamic Pottery," p. 26*, fig. 5:7–11.

28. Finkelstein, "Islamic Pottery," p. 28*, fig. 7:21; Magness, *Jerusalem Ceramic Chronology*, pp. 214, Casseroles Form 3.

29. Finkelstein, "Islamic Pottery," p. 28*, fig. 7:18; Avissar, "The Medieval Pottery," 132–35, Type 5. The Yoqneʿam examples differ, however, in their dark red brown ware, and the splashes of glaze suggest they are later than the Khirbet Abu Suwwana piece (which is of light orange ware and is apparently unglazed).

30. See Yosef Porath, "A Sixth–Seventh Century CE(?) Structure Near ʿEn ʿAneva," *ʿAtiqot* 42 (2001): 51*–56*, with an English-language summary on pp. 324–25.

Each unit consisted of an inner room and an outer room or courtyard, with the doorways opening from the outer rooms or courtyards onto a path that led to the spring and the riverbed.[31] All of the floors of the building were made of packed earth laid over a fill. Both of the outer rooms or courtyards had low stone benches built along the northern wall.[32]

Porath distinguished two occupation levels: Stratum 2 (the earlier phase) and Stratum 1 (the later phase). A layer of marly dust mixed with pebbles that covered the floors of the Stratum 2 (earlier) building seems to have come from the collapse of the roof. This together with the paucity of finds from this level suggested to Porath that the original building was abandoned before it collapsed.[33] The Stratum 1 building reused the earlier structure. The northern unit was reoccupied and the floor levels were raised. The bench in the outer room was put out of use.[34] The southern unit showed evidence of two sub-phases. In the earlier sub-phase (1B), the two rooms were united into one (L107). During this sub-phase, the building apparently consisted of one dwelling unit (the northern half of the building with the inner and outer rooms) and a large courtyard (or pen? = L107). Because no doorway was found in the wall between these two parts of the building (the dwelling and courtyard or pen), access would have been from the outside.[35] In the later sub-phase (1A), L107 (the southern unit) was redivided into two parts, along the lines of the original plan.[36]

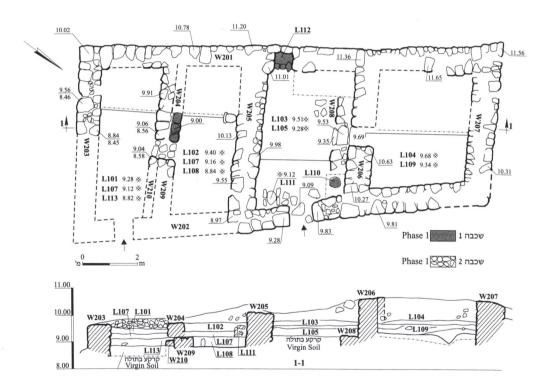

Figure 1.2. Plan of the building at Ein ʿAneva (from Yosef Porath, "A Sixth-Seventh Century C.E.(?) Structure Near ʿEn ʿAneva," *ʿAtiqot* 42 [2001]: plan 1; reprinted with permission of the Israel Antiquities Authority)

31. Porath, "ʿEn ʿAneva," p. 51*.

32. Porath, "ʿEn ʿAneva," p. 53*.

33. Porath, "ʿEn ʿAneva," p. 53*.

34. Porath, "ʿEn ʿAneva," p. 53*.

35. Porath, "ʿEn ʿAneva," p. 53*.

36. Porath, "ʿEn ʿAneva," p. 53*.

Installations were discovered only in the northern unit, which is the better preserved part of the building. An oven (*tabun*) was sunk into the floor in the northeast corner of the outer room or courtyard of the northern unit. A niche that apparently served as a cupboard was built into the wall at the southwest corner of the same room.[37] The floors of the Stratum 1 building (last occupation phase) were covered with a layer of fine, marly dust covered by large fieldstones. This indicates that the Stratum 1 occupation, like Stratum 2, ended with the abandonment and eventual collapse of the building.[38] Porath concluded that the plan of the building and its location next to agricultural fields indicate that it served a "civil," not military function.[39]

According to Porath, the few finds recovered do not provide an accurate date since they have a range from the second to eighth centuries C.E. He tentatively dated the structure to the sixth to seventh century, suggesting that it served as an agricultural plot for the Byzantine monastery at Masada beginning in the early sixth century and was deserted "some time after the Islamic conquest of the country in the mid-seventh century."[40] However, an examination of the finds indicates that the occupation dates to the early Islamic period.

Only seven finds — six fragments of ceramic vessels and a steatite bowl — are illustrated from the excavations (see fig. 1.3). The only pieces published from a Stratum 2 context are a cooking pot and the lower half of a jug.[41] The cooking pot represents a type that is well known from early Islamic contexts, and in my opinion, it should be dated mainly to the eighth century.[42] The rest of the published material comes from Stratum 1 contexts. The finds include a deep casserole, two casserole lids, and the rim and shoulder of a flask.[43] Though none of these types is closely datable, they could all be early Islamic. However, the steatite bowl, which comes from a Stratum 1A context in L102 of the southern unit, undoubtedly dates to the eighth to ninth centuries.[44] The coarseness of the bowl, the ledge handles, and the signs of burning indicate that it was used as a cooking vessel.[45] The occupation at Ein ʿAneva should therefore be dated to the eighth to ninth centuries. As Porath noted, a great deal of effort was invested in the establishment of this small agricultural holding, including the construction of terraces on the very steep bank of Nahal Zeelim. The terraces were watered by a channel or aqueduct that brought water from the nearby spring.[46] Interestingly, although we know that the Roman army utilized the water from the spring at Ein ʿAneva during the siege of Masada, the only evidence for permanent settlement and exploitation of the spring is during the early Islamic period.

MODULAR ARCHITECTURE

Porath noted the peculiar arrangement of identical side-by-side units at Ein ʿAneva, each consisting of an inner room and outer room or courtyard.[47] These modular units — which have been described elsewhere as "nucleus units" by Mordechai Haiman[48] — are characteristic of

---

37. Porath, "ʿEn ʿAneva," p. 53*.

38. Porath, "ʿEn ʿAneva," p. 53*.

39. Porath, "ʿEn ʿAneva," p. 324.

40. Porath, "ʿEn ʿAneva," p. 324.

41. Porath, "ʿEn ʿAneva," p. 53*, fig. 2:4–5 (for their context see table on p. 54*).

42. The cooking pot is illustrated in Porath, "ʿEn ʿAneva," p. 53*, fig. 2:4. For parallels see Rina Avner, "Elat-Elot: An Early Islamic Village," ʿAtiqot 36 (1998): 32*, fig. 13:8–10 (in Hebrew).

43. Porath, "ʿEn ʿAneva," p. 53*, fig. 2:1–3, 6.

44. See Jodi Magness, "The Dating of the Black Ceramic Bowl with a Depiction of the Torah Shrine from Nabratein," *Levant* 26 (1994): 199–206.

45. Porath, "ʿEn ʿAneva," p. 54*.

46. Porath, "ʿEn ʿAneva," p. 55*.

47. Porath, "ʿEn ʿAneva," p. 55*. According to Porath, it is not characteristic of Palestine.

48. Mordechai Haiman, "Agriculture and Nomad-State Relations in the Negev Desert in the Byzantine and Early Islamic Periods," *Bulletin of the American Schools of Oriental Research* 297 (1995): 35.

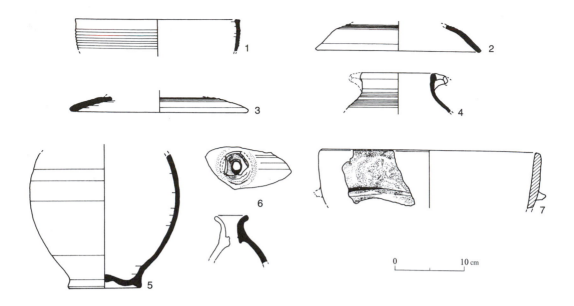

Figure 1.3. Pottery and stone bowl from Ein ʿAneva (from Yosef Porath, "A Sixth-Seventh Century
C.E.(?) Structure Near ʿEn ʿAneva," *ʿAtiqot* 42 [2001]: fig. 2; reprinted with
permission of the Israel Antiquities Authority)

some early Islamic villages and farmhouses in Palestine. They are attested, for example, in the
eighth to ninth century village excavated by Rina Avner at Eilat-Eilot and at other villages in the
Eilat region.[49] The rooms were constructed according to recurring measurements, with external
dimensions ranging from about three to five meters.[50] The dimensions reflect the maximum
length of the wooden beams that could be obtained for roofing. The floors are of beaten earth,
and the walls are constructed of stone or mudbrick on a stone socle. The rooms are arranged as
side-by-side units, sometimes with narrow rooms or courtyards between them. The buildings in
the Eilat area villages and at Ein ʿAneva are aligned along the banks of wadis.

At Khirbet Abu Suwwana, we see a variation on this modular arrangement. The dwellings
consist again of side-by-side units, sometimes with rows of single rooms and sometimes two
rooms, one behind another. These units are clustered around a series of courtyards or common
open spaces. Here too the units are aligned according to the topography, running roughly north-
south along the slope of the hill.[51]

A number of scholars have commented on the appearance of this type of modular architecture in early Islamic Palestine. For example, Uzi Avner and Jodi Magness note that, "The degree
of uniformity among the buildings in the six villages [in the Eilat region] suggests a common ar-

49. See R. Avner, "Elat-Elot," p. 33*; idem, "Eilat,"
    Hadashot Arkheologiyot 103 (1995), and 105 (in
    Hebrew). For the other villages in the Eilat region,
    see Uzi Avner and Jodi Magness, "Early Islamic
    Settlement in the Southern Negev," *Bulletin of the
    American Schools of Oriental Research* 310
    (1998): 40. For an example near Sde Boqer, see

    Rudolph Cohen, *Archaeological Survey of Israel,
    Map of Sede Boqer-East (168), 13–03* (Jerusalem,
    1981), p. 51, plan 2 (Nahal HaRoʿah).
50. U. Avner and Magness, "Early Islamic Settlement,"
    p. 40.
51. Sion, "Khirbet Abu Suwwana," p. 186.

chitectural experience and social organization."[52] They have suggested that this uniformity reflects the initiative of a single body that organized or sponsored the settlement of one or more ethnic groups.[53] Haiman points out that the Negev farmhouses also show this combination of modular units. The farmhouses consist of one or more square buildings, each with one to three rooms and a courtyard.[54] Each of these units seems to reflect a dwelling structure for a family of four or five individuals. Haiman believes that each farm was jointly owned by a group of families, analogous to a Bedouin "paternal house."[55]

Relatively small, square, or rectangular rooms have always been a characteristic component of rural architecture in Palestine due to the limited availability of wooden beams for roofing. However, the modular units of the early Islamic villages and farms are arranged in a different manner from those of the Roman and Byzantine periods, suggesting a change in the organization of familial units (and perhaps therefore in the origins of the inhabitants) and in the village structure. Yizhar Hirschfeld establishes a typology of the private dwellings of Roman and Byzantine Palestine based on their layout.[56] He distinguishes three main types of houses based on differences in ground plans:

1. The simple house: The most basic and common Roman/Byzantine dwelling type consists of a one or two room house behind or in front of an open courtyard.[57]

2. The complex house: This is an expanded version of the simple house by means of wings or dwelling units built around three or more sides of the outer courtyard.[58]

3. The courtyard house: This dwelling type has a central courtyard surrounded by rooms on all four sides. According to Hirschfeld, this house-type was used exclusively by wealthy families and is usually found in cities.[59]

The common denominator of all of these dwelling types is the arrangement of rooms around or along one or more sides of an open courtyard. In villages such as Capernaum, Chorazin, and Khirbet Sumaqa, the houses are grouped together in insulae separated by streets or alleys.[60] Sometimes large houses can take up an entire insula, as at Mampsis.[61]

The early Islamic villages and farms that we have considered here follow the long-established local tradition of having one or more rooms built along one or more sides of an open courtyard. However, they also display significant differences. One of the most striking features is the repetition of relatively small rooms, all roughly the same size in each dwelling and occur-

---

52. U. Avner and Magness, "Early Islamic Settlement," p. 40.

53. U. Avner and Magness, "Early Islamic Settlement," p. 40.

54. Haiman "Agriculture," p. 41.

55. Haiman "Agriculture," p. 41.

56. Yizhar Hirschfeld, *The Palestinian Dwelling in the Roman-Byzantine Period* (Jerusalem, 1995).

57. Hirschfeld, *Palestinian Dwelling*, p. 21.

58. Hirschfeld, *Palestinian Dwelling*, p. 22.

59. Hirschfeld, *Palestinian Dwelling*, p. 22, 102. Atrium or peristyle houses, a sub-type of the courtyard house, are rare in Palestine; see ibid., pp. 57, 85–97.

60. For Capernaum, see Stanislao Loffreda, *Recovering Capharnaum* (Jerusalem, 1985), pp. 8–9; for Chorazim, see Zeʾev Yevin, *The Synagogue at Korazim: The 1962–1964 and 1980–1987 Excavations* (Israel Antiquities Authority Reports 10; Jerusalem, 2000), p. 5, plan 2; for Sumaqa, see Shimon Dar, *Sumaqa: A Roman and Byzantine Jewish Village on Mount Carmel, Israel* (British Archaeological Reports, International Series 815; Oxford, 1999), p. 15, map 3; p. 36, fig. 20. The streets or alleys are not always laid out orthogonally.

61. See Arthur Segal, *The Byzantine City of Shivta (Esbeita), Negev Desert, Israel* (British Archaeological Reports, International Series 179; Oxford, 1983), p. 63, fig. 19; Hirschfeld, *Palestinian Dwelling*, pp. 73–76.

ring throughout the settlement. There is no evidence for a second story level, which is a common (though not universal) feature of all types of Palestinian Roman-Byzantine dwellings.[62] Although the number of units in each early Islamic house differs, the rooms do not vary greatly in size and are not differentiated in other ways, such as by interior decoration. Each dwelling consists of one or more side-by-side rooms (sometimes with two rooms, one behind the other). These rooms include working areas with tabuns and other installations, which might have been small open courtyards. The rooms are aligned along an open space that may have provided access to more than one familial unit. The units can be contiguous or separated by some distances, but there are no insulae. Hirschfeld has noted that in Roman-Byzantine villages in Palestine, the poorer artisans and farmers typically occupied much smaller houses on the periphery of the settlement.[63] In contrast, there is no clear differentiation in dwelling size or elaboration within these early Islamic settlements and no indication that poorer families were spatially marginalized within the village.

Haiman's suggestion that the introduction of this type of modular architecture can be understood as reflecting the structure of a Bedouin paternal house is attractive. The smallest units of the Bedouin tribal system consist of small individual families or clans that migrate and camp together. Werner Caskel has observed that, "In this tribal organism there was no official leader, let alone a hierarchy. A leader can acquire a position of any official character only by being appointed to, or confirmed in, his office by a non-Bedouin power; otherwise he is only a *primus inter pares*."[64] Caskel notes that this tribal organization and its ideological superstructure are found not only among the Bedouins but also among settled Muslim populations.[65] The modular architecture seems to reflect the kind of social structure described by Caskel. Its appearance may therefore provide evidence for the settlement of a new or different ethnic group (or groups).

Another interesting difference between the Byzantine and early Islamic villages that we have considered is the placement of the religious (congregational) buildings. Generally speaking, in Byzantine villages, the synagogues and churches (aside from monastic establishments) tend to occupy a central position within the settlement. In contrast, at Khirbet Abu Suwwana the mosque is at the edge of the village, and nearly all of the mosques in the Negev highlands are located outside the settlement, often on a hilltop a few dozen meters away.[66] Exceptions to this rule include the mosques in settlements such as Khirbet Susiya, Eshtemoa (Samoʿa), and Shivta, where an earlier church or synagogue was converted into a mosque. Perhaps this too reflects a different kind of social organization and structure within the village. Placing the congregational religious structure in the center of the village requires the appropriation of communal property and therefore some sort of organizing authority. The location of mosques may also represent a different religious tradition. For example, if we assume that these villages were occupied by families or clans structured like subunits of Bedouin tribes, which were accustomed to worship at open-air shrines, it may have been important to place the religious congregational structure next to or in an open space.

62. See Hirschfeld, *Palestinian Dwelling*, p. 102.

63. Hirschfeld, *Palestinian Dwelling*, p. 68.

64. Werner Caskel, "The Bedouinization of Arabia," in *The Arabs and Arabia on the Eve of Islam*, edited by Frank E. Peters (Aldershot, 1999), p. 35.

65. Caskel, "Bedouinization," p. 36.

66. See Gideon Avni, "Early Mosques in the Negev Highlands: New Archaeological Evidence on Islamic Penetration of Southern Palestine," *Bulletin of the American Schools of Oriental Research* 294 (1994): 83–100.

I believe that we see here at a micro-level (i.e., the level of the family and village) the same sort of changes that have been noted by Hugh Kennedy at the macro-level (the level of the town or *madina*).[67] The classical cities of the Near East were characterized by an orthogonal layout with broad colonnaded streets and large open agoras or forums surrounded by monumental public buildings. In contrast, during the early Islamic period, city streets were frequently converted into narrow, private, cul-de-sacs giving access to the houses on each side. The open spaces of the agoras were replaced by suqs, with shops lining narrow streets or alleys. Large markets were now located outside the gates, where livestock could be brought from the countryside for sale.[68] Mosques not only replaced churches as religious buildings, but also agoras, theaters, and civic basilicas in the functional sense of serving as public congregational structures.[69]

Kennedy attributes these changes to a number of factors. For example, the system of patronage changed. Whereas in the classical cities the emperor and his local representatives sponsored the construction of public monuments, the Muslim state authorities interfered less in the activities of their subjects. Although the Umayyads constructed some large urban mosques and rural palaces, they did not spend money beautifying the streets of cities or on public entertainment.[70] In addition, whereas Roman law made a sharp distinction between state and private property, in Islamic law the important unit was the family and its house.[71] On the other hand, I disagree with Kennedy's assertion that "commerce and manufacture do not seem to have been the most important factor in the prosperity of [classical] towns."[72] According to Kennedy, classical towns derived their prosperity from the activities of neighboring landowners who chose to live in them. In contrast, Islamic towns, with their narrow streets lined with small shops, "brought the focus of commercial activity firmly within the city walls."[73] Kennedy believes that one consequence of the change from open colonnaded streets to crowded suqs was to increase the number of retail shops inside the city.[74]

In my opinion, the difference between the classical city and the Islamic city is in the location, not the level of commercial activity. The agora or forum of a classical city functioned as its commercial center. Vendors set up their stalls and sold their wares in this large, open paved space, which was typically located in a central spot. Access was provided by broad streets, which were also lined by shops. The broad streets were necessary to accommodate wheeled carts and other wheeled traffic in which the goods were transported. Richard Bulliet suggests that broad colonnaded streets disappeared in early Islamic cities because wheeled transport was replaced by pack animals. Now camels, donkeys, and mules carried merchandise to small shops lining narrow streets and alleys. Large animals and fresh produce were offered for sale in large open areas outside the city walls.[75]

---

67. See Hugh Kennedy, "From *Polis* to *Madina*: Urban Changes in Late Antique and Early Islamic Syria," *Past and Present* 106 (1985): 3–27.

68. Kennedy, *Polis* to *Madina*, pp. 12–13. However, Kennedy notes that Muslim rulers adopted orthogonal town planning when laying out new cities. The difference is that whereas "in classical antiquity most cities including the largest and wealthiest were planned and ordered, in Islamic society they were not" (p. 16).

69. Kennedy, "*Polis* to *Madina*," pp. 15–16.

70. Kennedy, "*Polis* to *Madina*," pp. 18–20.

71. Kennedy, "*Polis* to *Madina*," p. 21.

72. Kennedy, "*Polis* to *Madina*," p. 23.

73. Kennedy, "*Polis* to *Madina*," p. 25.

74. Kennedy, "*Polis* to *Madina*," p. 25.

75. See Richard W. Bulliet, *The Camel and the Wheel* (Cambridge, 1975), especially pp. 224–28.

Khirbet Abu Suwwana, Ein ʿAneva, and other early Islamic villages and farms may provide evidence at the micro-level for the changes described by Kennedy. The Roman and Byzantine villages of Palestine had many of the same features of the larger towns and cities but on a more modest scale. These features include an orthogonal layout (sometimes), differentiation in the size and ornamentation of private dwellings (reflecting the existence of local elites), and the placement of market areas and public congregational buildings in the center of the settlement (due to the patronage or organizational impetus of local elites). In contrast, the early Islamic villages and farms we have considered here are characterized by modular architecture. Within each settlement, there is little differentiation in size and ornamentation. This organization seems to reflect a village structure oriented around the familial unit instead of powerful individuals or patrons belonging to local elites. The public congregational building, the mosque, was now located on the periphery of the village or outside it. The open spaces around the mosque might also have been the site of commerce and other public activities, like the markets outside the walls of cities where large animals and produce were sold.

Not all of the early Islamic settlements in Palestine — whether established *de novo* after the Muslim conquest or occupied continuously from the Roman/Byzantine period — have modular architecture or show no evidence for social differentiation. For example, an early Islamic house at Khirbet Susiya has two symmetrical wings with dwelling rooms opening onto a courtyard on one side and two small shops opening onto an alley on the other side. Hirschfeld notes parallels for this layout at Roman and Byzantine sites in Palestine.[76] In the early Islamic village at Capernaum there are discernible differences in the sizes of the houses and the sizes of the rooms within the houses.[77] The buildings in the village, many of which had a second story, lined broad lanes.[78] A large public building of unknown function appears to be located inside the village.[79] During the second phase of early Islamic occupation, many of the rooms inside the houses were subdivided or new rooms were added, and some of the streets were blocked.[80] A modest dwelling built in Tiberias during the ʿAbbasid period consists of two small, square side-by-side rooms opening onto a courtyard. Its ground plan looks modular, but unlike the examples from the village and farms we have considered, this house had a second story level with living quarters.[81] A large urban dwelling of the Umayyad period at Pella contained two peristyle courtyards, attesting to the continuity of this Roman/Byzantine building tradition.[82] The presence of six residential units described as being of "relatively high quality" in Area D at Khirbet Abu

---

76. See Hirschfeld, *Palestinian Dwelling*, pp. 37–38; idem, "Excavation of a Jewish Dwelling at Khirbet Susiya," *Eretz-Israel* 17 (1984): 168–80. For parallels at Beth Shearim and Gerasa, see p. 177 nn. 11–12. For the suggestion that this house was established in the early Islamic period and not during the sixth century, as Hirschfeld claims, see Jodi Magness, *The Archaeology of the Early Islamic Settlement in Palestine* (Winona Lake, 2003), pp. 101–02.

77. See Vassilios Tzaferis, *Excavations at Capernaum, Volume 1: 1978–1982* (Winona Lake, 1989), pp. 5–6 (Area C; perhaps a public building), 10–19 (Area A). According to Jodi Magness, "The Chronology of Capernaum in the Early Islamic Period," *Journal of the American Oriental Society* 117

(1997): 481–86, Stratum V should be dated ca. 700–750, and Stratum IV should be dated ca. 750 to the second half of the ninth century.

78. Tzaferis, *Capernaum*, pp. 15–16.

79. Tzaferis, *Capernaum*, p. 3 (Area B).

80. Tzaferis, *Capernaum*, pp. 16–19 (Area A).

81. See Hirschfeld, *Palestinian Dwelling*, pp. 40–42 and fig. 19; idem, "Tiberias," *Excavations and Surveys in Israel* 9 (1989/1990): 107–09.

82. See Anthony McNicoll, Robert H. Smith, and Basil Hennessy, *Pella in Jordan, Volume 1: An Interim Report on the Joint University of Sydney and the College of Wooster Excavations at Pella 1979–1981* (Canberra, 1982), pp. 123–26; Hirschfeld, *Palestinian Dwelling*, pp. 47–49.

Suwwana[83] suggests that there might have been some degree of social differentiation even in settlements with modular architecture. In other words, differences in the size, layout, and elaboration of houses, presumably reflecting social differentiation and the existence of elites within towns and villages, are discernible in many settlements in early Islamic Palestine.

The newly-established farms and villages with modular architecture — such as Khirbet Abu Suwwana and Ein ʿAneva — tend to be located on Palestine's desert periphery. The appearance of modular architecture in these farms and villages presumably reflects the settlement of a new population with a distinctive social organization and needs. As Hirschfeld notes, the manner in which private dwellings are designed regulates and even controls the lives of their inhabitants.[84] Similarly, at the macro-level Kennedy observes that city planning "was adapted for different purposes, life-styles, and legal customs. The changing aspect of the city was determined by long-term social, economic and cultural forces."[85] As we have seen, villages and farms with modular architecture may best be understood as reflecting a familial and village organization along tribal lines. Haiman argues that the establishment of new settlements in the desert periphery of Palestine during the Umayyad period is due to the deliberate, state-sponsored sedentarization of nomadic tribes.[86] Although I am not convinced that this process is the result of state sponsorship, Haiman is correct that the peripheral desert regions were settled only when there was a strong and stable government authority.[87]

In this paper, I have attempted to shift scholarly attention to small settlements in early Islamic Palestine's peripheral regions by focusing on the appearance of modular architecture. This complex phenomenon, which archaeology is uniquely positioned to illuminate, deserves more systematic treatment. For example, it would be instructive to document all known examples of settlements with modular architecture and examine their pattern of distribution relative to other settlements. The social structures of villages and small towns versus large towns and cities in the Roman/Byzantine and early Islamic periods need to be studied. Factors other than social and political structures should also be considered in relation to the appearance of modular architecture. Can this architecture be best understood in light of the settlement of a new population organized along tribal lines? Hopefully, future studies and new discoveries will provide us with additional information to help understand this phenomenon.

83. See Sion, "Khirbet Abu Suwwana."
84. Hirschfeld, *Palestinian Dwelling*, p. 15.
85. Kennedy, *"Polis* to *Madina,"* p. 17.

86. Haiman, "Agriculture," pp. 46–47.
87. Haiman, "Agriculture," pp. 46–47.

2

ASCALON ON THE LEVANTINE COAST

TRACY HOFFMAN

The issue of changing social identities in the Early Islamic period can be investigated on numerous levels; in the case of the medieval port city of Ascalon the question is best approached through a study of the city's urban development during the Byzantine and Early Islamic period.[1] This approach is rendered difficult by the nature of the archaeological record. Initially investigated by visitors such as the Comte de Forbin and Lady Hester Stanhope in the early nineteenth century, Ascalon was first excavated by John Garstang and his assistant W. Phythian Adams in the early twentieth century.[2] Their work uncovered evidence of architecture dating to the Islamic period and earlier scattered throughout the site. More recent excavations under the direction of Lawrence Stager have produced significant medieval period material culture ranging from architecture to ceramics.[3] The location and nature of this material makes the site of Ascalon so challenging and promising for the study of Islamic period cities and their inhabitants (fig. 2.1).

Traditionally, archaeologists have approached the study of Islamic period cities through an analysis of their institutions or vernacular architecture. Some practical reasons for this approach can be explained by the quality of preservation and the types of artifacts generally identified, and subsequently regarded, as providing the most direct evidence for change or development in a city. The construction of a mosque, for instance, in a city where none previously existed, reveals information not only about inhabitants of that community but also about the development of the given site. It also represents the type of visible change that draws scholarly attention. Indeed, modification on any level of the city center, generally the public heart of a city, often serves as the starting point for interpreting change generally, and in the framework of this study, transitions from the Byzantine to Early Islamic period more specifically. The lure of urban institutions is so powerful that it is seemingly impossible to interpret a city in their absence.[4] At a site such as Ascalon, where the limited evidence for city institutions stems largely from the identification of where they are not, it is necessary to develop a new methodology for interpreting the city.

At first glance, interpreting the city of Ascalon seems straightforward; the transition from the Byzantine to Early Islamic period and beyond appears to be well documented in limited but nonetheless informative references that illuminate important aspects of the city. Some of the most intriguing and as yet underutilized sources are Byzantine and Early Islamic period mosaic depictions of Ascalon, such as the Madaba Map and Umm al-Rasas, which show the *cardo*,

---

1. See Tracy Hoffman, "Ascalon 'Arus al-Sham: Domestic Architecture and the Development of a Byzantine-Islamic City" (Ph.D. diss., University of Chicago, 2003).

2. For the publication of preliminary results, see J. Garstang, "The Fund's Excavation of Askalon," *Palestine Exploration Quarterly* 21 (1921): 12–16; idem, "The Excavation of Askalon, 1920–1921," *Palestine Exploration Quarterly* 21 (1921): 73–75; idem, "The Excavations at Askalon," *Palestine Exploration Quarterly* 22 (1922): 112–19; idem,

"Askalon," *Palestine Exploration Quarterly* 24 (1924): 24–35.

3. Lawrence Stager, *Ashkelon Discovered: From Canaanites and Philistines to Romans and Moslems* (Washington, D.C., 1991).

4. The literature on the subject of Islamic cities and their institutions is extensive and devoid of any consensus on matters of definition. A good synopsis of some of the main issues can be found in Timothy Insoll, *The Archaeology of Islam* (Oxford, 1999).

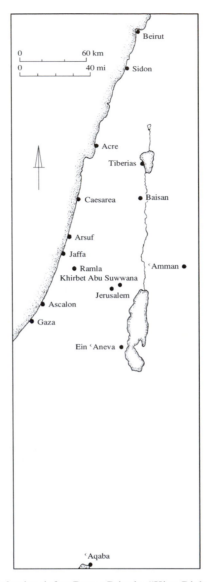

Figure 2.1. Map of Palestine (after Denys Pringle, "King Richard I and the Walls of
Ascalon," *Palestine Exploration Quarterly* 116 [1984]: pl. 1)

decumanus, a city gate, multistory buildings, and the main church in the late sixth century (fig.
2.2).[5] In these mosaics the public face, the monumental vernacular architecture, of a classical
city is easily recognizable. They also show aspects of the city infrastructure such as streets and
fortifications that in addition to the various buildings depicted may be identifiable in the archaeological record.

---

5. Herbert Donner, *The Mosaic Map of Madaba: An
    Introductory Guide* (Kampen, 1992); Michèle
    Piccirillo, and Eugenio Alliata, eds., *The Madaba
    Map Centenary, 1897–1997: Travelling through the
    Byzantine Umayyad Period* (Proceedings of the In-
    ternational Conference Held in Amman, 7–9 April

1997; Jerusalem, 1999). A third mosaic depicts
what is identified as the central church of Ascalon,
refer to Roland de Vaux, "Une mosaïque byzantine
à Ma'in (Transjordanie)," *Revue Biblique* 47
(1938): 227–58.

Descriptions found in texts that constitute the written record on medieval Ascalon also focus on the city's public institutions.[6] Dating from the tenth century and later these texts describe institutions that differ from those depicted in the mosaics, referring instead to the city mosque and suqs rather than Ascalon churches. One of the most well-known descriptions is Muqaddasi's commentary in the tenth century on Ascalon's mosque, thriving markets, strong fortifications, and unusable harbor.[7] A century later Nasir-i Khusraw mentions the city's multistory buildings.[8] Sporadic details about Ascalon in other texts include a brief mention of the city mosque by Usamah ibn-Munqidh in the twelfth century. Perhaps the most vivid description is William of Tyre's recording of the Crusader siege of Ascalon in 1153 C.E., which offers the most detailed description of the city's fortifications and the surrounding area. In general, the sources describe a thriving city with the expected markers, suqs, and mosques of an Islamic city. In many ways the information is the same as that found in the mosaic depictions; city institutions are enumerated, even as much of the city remains unilluminated.

These sources add few details to the history of Ascalon as a city that is known to have surrendered to Mu'awiya on terms (*sulhan*) in the mid-seventh century.[9] Situated on the southern Levantine coast, a border with the Byzantine controlled Mediterranean, Ascalon, along with other port cities, was the focus of efforts to settle new inhabitants in and around the city to bolster its defenses and that of the expanding Islamic empire. In due course sources record the construction of a mint and a mosque in Ascalon although it is not until the descriptions outlined above that any real picture of the city emerges. Passing from Umayyad to 'Abbasid and then Tulunid rule Ascalon's ties with Egypt were cemented under the Fatimids. William of Tyre's description indicates the importance Ascalon held for both the Fatimids and Crusaders during the twelfth century from which time the city traded hands repeatedly until it was ultimately abandoned in the mid-thirteenth century. Documentary sources on Ascalon illuminate, in however limited a way, the most useful aspects of the city for tracing change and continuity, but the sources do not reveal everything. In fact, the only way to assess the development of the city is through the archaeological record and what it might reveal about the events, institutions, and inhabitants as seen in the documentary evidence.

Since 1985 the Leon Levy Ashkelon Expedition has conducted the first large-scale systematic excavation of the ancient city housed within the remains of the medieval city wall (fig. 2.3). In an effort to best target the time periods of interest, the Canaanite and Philistine periods, the expedition has explored and/or excavated the three mounds, designated North, Middle, and South, as well as the ground level areas that constitute the site of ancient Ascalon. In the process,

6. For a summary of the medieval sources that describe Ascalon, see Moshe Sharon, *Egyptian Caliph and English Baron: The Story of an Arabic Inscription from Ashkelon* (Corpus Inscriptionum Arabicarum Palaestinae; Jerusalem, 1994).

7. Muḥammad ibn Ahmed Muqaddasi, *Ahsan al-taqāsīm fi ma'rifat al-aqālīm*, edited by M. J. de Geoje (Bibliotheca Geographorum Arabicorum 3; Leiden, 1906), p. 174.

8. Nasir-i Khusraw, Nasir-i Khusraw's *Book of Travels*, edited and translated by Wheeler M. Thackston (Costa Mesa, 2001); Usāmah ibn-Munqidh, *An Arab-Syrian Gentleman and Warrior in the Period of the Crusades: Memoirs of Usāmah ibn-Munqidh*, translated by Philip K. Hitti (Records of Civiliza-

tion, Sources and Studies 10; New York, 1929), p. 40; William of Tyre, *A History of Deeds Done Beyond the Sea*, translated by Emily Atwater Babcock and August Charles Krey (Records of Civilization, Sources and Studies 35; New York, 1943).

9. For the history of Ascalon in the medieval period, refer to Moshe Sharon, *Corpus Inscriptionum Arabicarum Palaestinae*, Volume 1: *A* (Leiden, 1997); see also Pringle, "King Richard I and the Walls of Ascalon," pp. 133–47; J. Prawer, "Ascalon and the Ascalon Strip in Crusader Politics," *Eretz Israel* 4 (1956): 231–48 (Hebrew with English summary), and "The City and Duchy of Ascalon in the Crusader Period," *Eretz Israel* 5 (1958): 224–37.

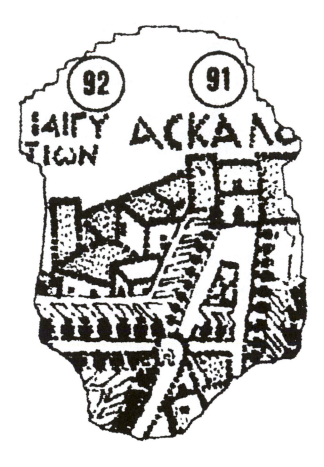

Figure 2.2. Ascalon in the Madaba map (after Donner, *The Mosaic Map of Madaba*)

a large corpus of Byzantine and Islamic period material culture was collected, establishing a scattered but viable database for analyzing the city. Conspicuously absent from the archaeological record, however, is any evidence for city institutions; the very images that pervade the documentary evidence are absent from a material record that is largely non-public in nature. The archaeological record can in any case be used to trace the development of the city and how that process might have affected the city's inhabitants.

The material record of Ascalon from the Byzantine and Early Islamic periods consists chiefly of five buildings identified as domestic structures, a church, and a kiln housed in the converted remains of an earlier bath house. At least two more structures, another bath and a second kiln, originally constructed in the Roman period continued to be used into the Byzantine period. An examination of these structures reveals a remarkable degree of continuity as well as visible change in the housing, organization, and plan of the city. Although non-public in nature the archaeological evidence for Ascalon provides an opportunity not only to examine this aspect of the city but also to explore its potential in dealing with the larger issues of urban development and changing social identities.

The excavated domestic structures cluster on the three mounds with the notable exception of one building that is located just under the city wall. Starting on the North mound, Structure One is situated near the city gate and in proximity to two other buildings, a church and a bath (fig.

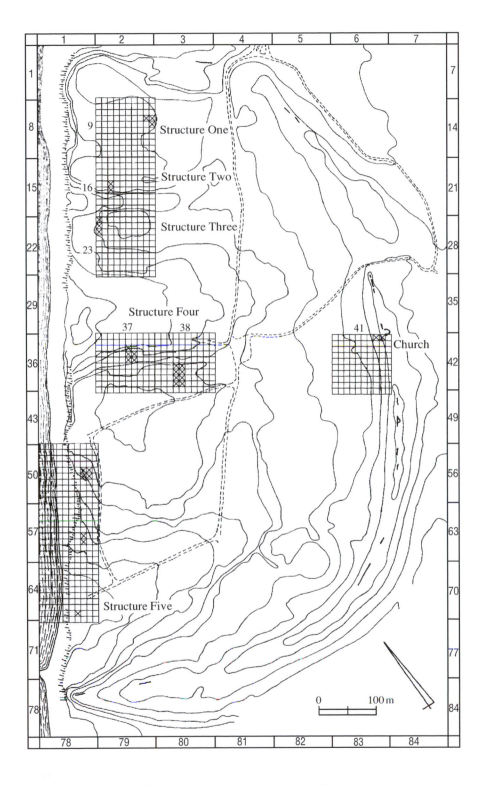

Figure 2.3. Excavation areas in Ascalon

2.4). While the latter two buildings predate the house in their construction, the evidence is in-conclusive as to whether or not the three buildings might have had some overlapping periods of use. As a building, a number of characteristics or features in Structure One appear to be common in houses throughout the city. The plan consists of a central courtyard around which three rooms can be identified. The standard building material for both interior and exterior walls is stone with both uncut fieldstones and cut ashlar blocks present. The flooring materials range from beaten earth and plaster surfaces in interior rooms to stone paving in the courtyard. A prominent feature in this house is a drainage system that includes three intakes and a main channel which starts in the courtyard then branches into two channels into two of the interior rooms.

One may note that at least part of the structure was built prior to the Byzantine and Early Is-lamic periods, a conclusion that is based on stratigraphy and the analysis of ceramics collected during the excavation of certain walls. The existing segment of the building continued to be used during subsequent periods of renovation and occupation. Ceramics collected from within the house and analysis of the architectural remains indicate this structure continued to be used into the Middle Islamic period and in all probability through the final occupation of the city in the mid-thirteenth century. The longevity of the use of this structure is noteworthy as is the realiza-tion that the maintenance and any renovation of the building did not result in significant organizational or functional changes.

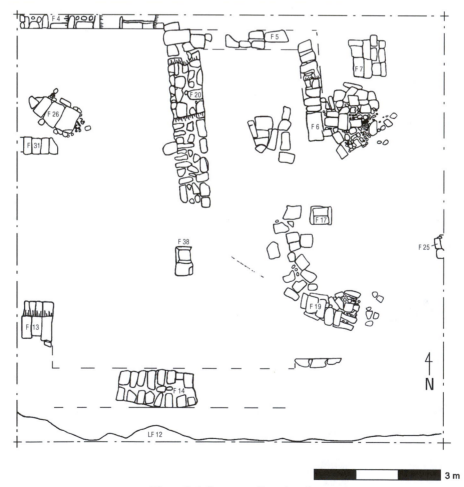

Figure 2.4. Structure One. Ascalon

As an independent building Structure One demonstrates the types of building materials and features as well as the type of building layout that might be found in the houses of Ascalon. It further indicates that houses might be located near non-domestic structures such as baths and churches, and that prolonged periods of use were common for some of the buildings in Ascalon. In this area of the city then, the North mound, the nature of the architectural evidence illuminates not only the nature of the city's housing but also the organization of Ascalon's neighborhoods.

The evidence from Structure Two, located south of Structure One on the North mound, is more elusive but deserves some mention because of its location (fig. 2.5). The remains of this structure, also identified as a house, are fragmentary and consist chiefly of a number of stone walls that form at least two rooms. Five meters away from the main structure is a plaster floor in which are two stone-lined fire pits. The stratigraphic evidence indicates that the main building and this surface were probably used contemporaneously, but it is impossible to determine whether or not it is all part of one building.

Again, features first seen in Structure One such as stone walls and beaten earth surfaces are visible in this house. One distinctive aspect of this second house is that it does not have as long a period of use as Structure One. Although the fragmentary nature of the architecture and material culture collected from Structure Two makes it difficult to provide a firm chronology, it seems clear that this house was used only in the Byzantine and Early Islamic periods. Unlike many other houses in Ascalon, no evidence indicates that it was occupied into the Middle Islamic period. Any assessment of this house must acknowledge that it does not offer much new material in terms of the physical structure of the building. The paucity of the building's remains does not detract from the significance of its location, and its existence more generally, which serves to demonstrate the extent of settlement within the city. Together, Structures One and Two indicate that much of the North mound was settled and that much of that occupation was residential in nature.

Farther to the south the Middle mound has a third building (Structure Three), one of the largest and most complex structures dated to the Byzantine and Early Islamic periods (fig. 2.6). Structure Three reflects many of the patterns identified in the previously discussed houses while also showing some significant differences. The building materials are consistent with other buildings: stone walls and beaten earth, plaster, or stone paved surfaces, although some new features occur such as mosaic floors. This house has an extensive drainage system, which includes a well, with channels running through both interior and exterior spaces. The layout seems to consist of rooms around a courtyard although in this case the evidence argues for the existence of several courtyards and suites of rooms, indicating that this house might have functioned as a multiunit building. Indeed, the maze of rooms makes little sense as a single structure, but when viewed as a multiunit house, a form known to have existed in Ascalon, the architecture becomes more intelligible (see below).

Structure Three provides the most complete evidence for the reuse of a building constructed in the Byzantine period that underwent subsequent renovation and continued in use into the Middle Islamic period. The layout of the building changes substantially; part of the building is abandoned and the remainder of the structure reduced to one living unit. However, little evidence suggests that the modifications in the layout resulted in any changes in the overall function of the building. Structure Three appears to have been constructed as a house and to have been used as such while it was occupied. Interestingly, evidence for a second structure just to the north of Structure Three hints at the extent of settlement in this area of the city. The façade of this second building, less than one meter away, is pierced by a number of windows and appears to have an east–west dimension similar to that of Structure Three. Although the two

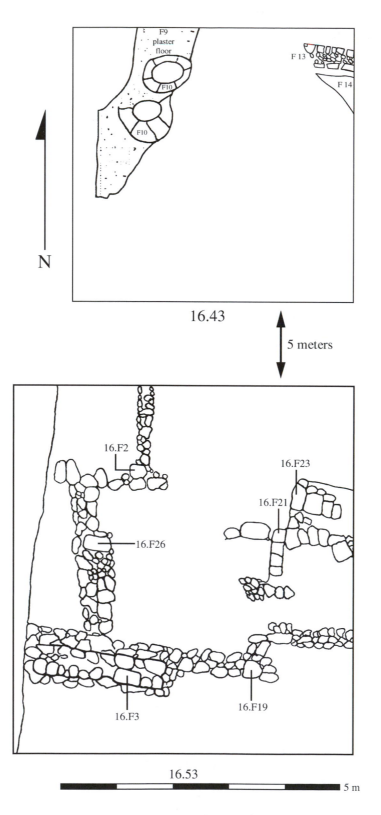

Figure 2.5. Structure Two. Ascalon

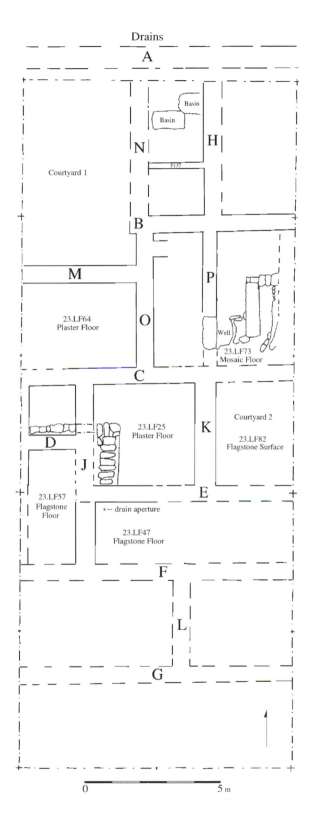

Figure 2.6. Structure Three, Phase 3. Ascalon

buildings are in close proximity, their constructions and placements are neither haphazard nor random; in this area of Ascalon the impression is one of deliberate planning rather than indiscriminate utilization of usable space.

Structure Four is located on the northern edge of the South mound (fig. 2.7). This building is clearly recognizable as a house with suites of rooms organized around a central courtyard. Structure Four displays many of the features found in other excavated houses. The building material is stone, and floors range from beaten earth or plaster to stone pavement and mosaic surfaces. An elaborate drainage system can also be associated with a small pool located in the courtyard. As in the case of Structures One and Two, evidence shows that part of Structure Four was built prior to the Islamic period. Analysis of the ceramics collected from the building's walls indicates that all the exterior walls date to the Byzantine period while the interior walls can be assigned an Early Islamic date. Some Byzantine period interior walls continued to be used in the Islamic period, indicating at least part of the existing organization of the building was maintained. This pattern of renovation and reuse is noteworthy as it occurs in other houses at Ascalon.

The longevity of this house is surprising since a number of new structures were built in its immediate vicinity. One of these new buildings with a courtyard and a pool of similar construction utilizes one of Structure Four's exterior walls. An additional building to the east shows that Structure Four was probably part of a densely settled neighborhood. The impression of this area is not the same one of deliberateness or orderliness as was seen in the area of Structure Three. Rather, the addition of new buildings, using in some cases walls of the existing structure, gives more of an impression of unregulated growth. Farther to the south, even greater change in this neighborhood is indicated as a former bath house, used into the Byzantine period, was converted into a kiln facility in the Early Islamic period (fig. 2.8). The continuity visible in Structure Four stands in striking contrast to the changes and developments in the buildings around this central structure.

If Structure Four is located in an area showing the densest occupation in Ascalon, then the last house, Structure Five, is in the most isolated area (fig. 2.9). Situated in the southwest corner of the city, just below the mound of the city's fortifications, the fragmentary remains of this house are located near the presumed area of the city's sea gate. The building consists of a series of walls that bound a courtyard with a well and an elaborate series of drains. In general this building displays the same building materials and the same features found in previously discussed houses. The ceramic evidence indicates a relatively short occupation and abandonment during the Early Islamic period. Structure Five is valuable as evidence for the extent and nature of settlement within the city walls, offering tangible proof that residential architecture, in at least some areas, extended up to the city walls and was not limited to the three mounds within the city. In addition, Structure Five is not the only building built near Ascalon's fortified city wall. Just south of the Jerusalem Gate is a Byzantine period church that continued to be used into the Middle Islamic period (fig. 2.10). Again, some of the greatest significance of this building lies in its location and what it reveals about the city plan.

This brief overview not only highlights some very important aspects of the housing at Ascalon but also illustrates development of the city plan. Basic patterns are repeated in each structure, such as similar building materials, features, and layouts, suggesting reuse without systematic reorganization during renovation. As many of the houses were built in part or in whole prior to the Islamic period, similarities and continuity in those aspects of the structures are obvious. Indeed, the longevity of the excavated houses indicates that in non-public areas of the city the status quo was maintained to a surprising degree. Partly, the answer lies in expediency; it

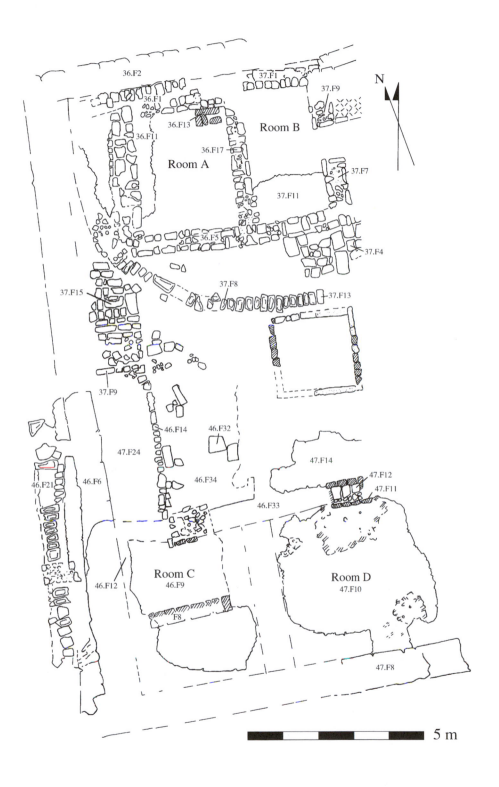

Figure 2.7. Structure Four. Ascalon

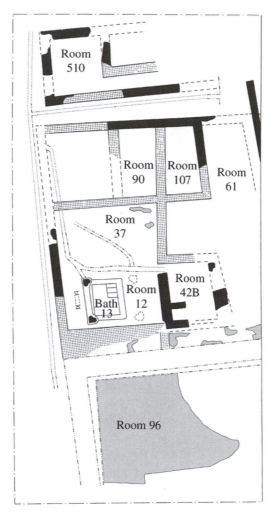

Scale 1:200

Figure 2.8. Grid 38 bath house. Ascalon

was easy to occupy standing buildings in good repair and the houses were a recognizable form, something in which the inhabitants of Ascalon — both old and new — were comfortable.

It would be misleading, however, to characterize the archaeological record as devoid of change, which is indicated both in the functions of buildings, such as the bath converted into a kiln, and in settlement, such as the construction of new buildings in the area of Structure Four. The significant drawback in understanding these changes lies in the nature of the archaeological record because they are so few and dispersed throughout the city. To make sense of the changes and to utilize the archaeological evidence to its full potential, additional context is needed so that these structures can be situated within the cityscape and made more meaningful. The situation of the structures in the cityscape is particularly important in trying to assess the Byzantine and Early Islamic period transition and in trying to understand what the city reflects about its inhabitants.

That much needed context is found in a little-known legal text, *On the Laws or Customs of Palestine*, which follows in a long tradition of texts written to govern both building practices and

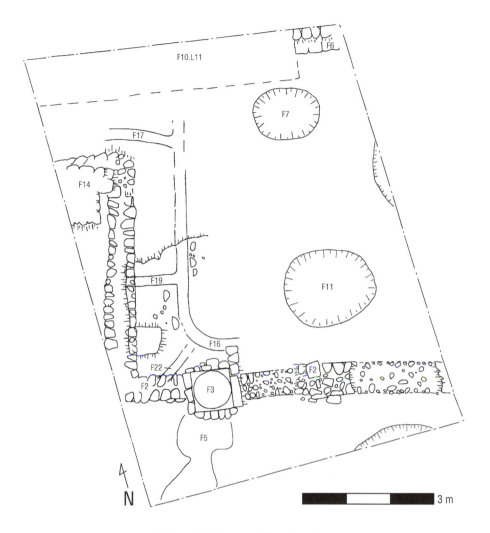

Figure 2.9. Structure Five. Ascalon

relations between neighbors stemming from such issues.[10] This volume is particularly useful in that it was written specifically about Ascalon. It is generally believed that the author of this code, an architect by the name of Julian, was born in the city of Ascalon and that he was still living there when he compiled the legal code during the mid-sixth century.[11] It is not known whether the compilation of the legal code was an officially sanctioned project or if it was an un-

10. Catherine Saliou, "Le Traité de Droit Urbain de Julien d'Ascalon: Coutumier et Codification," in *La codification des lois dans l'antiquité* (Actes du colloque de Strasbourg 27–29 Novembre, 1997), edited by Edmond Lévy (Travaux du centre de recherche sur le Proche-Orient et la Grèce antiques 16; Paris, 2000), pp. 293–313.

11. The origins of his family, whether they were pagan or Christian, are unclear. About Julian specifically, many scholars believe he had at least some classical education based on the fact that his text is written in Greek and that Julian makes reference to several classical authors. For the most complete discussion of Julian, his identity, and the dates of his text, see Joseph Geiger, "Julian of Ascalon," *Journal of Hellenic Studies* 112 (1992): 31–43. For a synopsis of Julian, which also discusses his origins, see Besim Hakim, "Julian of Ascalon's Treatise of Construction and Design Rules from Sixth Century Palestine," *Journal of the Society of Architectural Historians* 60 (2001): 4–25.

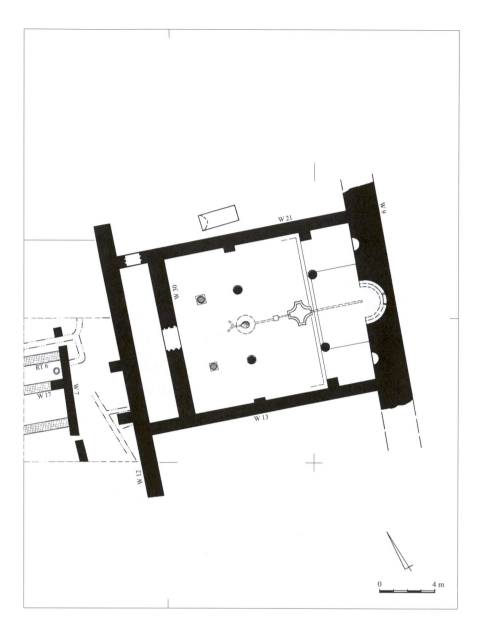

Figure 2.10. Church near Jerusalem gate. Ascalon

official endeavor on the part of a private citizen.[12] The motivation behind the writing of the treatise is equally unclear although scholars agree one reason was Julian's desire to ensure Ascalon
remained a pleasant place to live. This condition was achieved by minimizing the dangers and or
nuisances that certain activities or neighbors might cause each other and by preserving aesthetically pleasing aspects of the city, such as views, public art, and gardens.

Absent from Julian's text is any real reference to the city center or the public institutions of
the city, which suggests another possible explanation for his legal code. While construction and

---

12. On the subject of legal codes in this period and the
various schools of thought that might have influenced Julian, see Hakim, "Julian of Ascalon," pp.
6–8.

renovation in public areas of the city remained well regulated, perhaps the same was not true for such practices in non-public areas of the city. In simple terms, perhaps the text was necessary, perhaps it met a need generated by the inhabitants of Ascalon who were neglecting traditional principles of design and construction in the classical city, thereby producing an unpleasant urban environment. Perhaps the pace and/or nature of change within the built environment, even if well controlled, was significant enough for a need to reiterate regulations on a more intimate level than the legal code issued in Constantinople. Julian never states why he compiled the legal code, but it is nonetheless significant that in the mid-sixth century such a code was written for Ascalon. Equally significant, its inclusion in the mid-fourteenth century *Hexabiblos* of Constantine Harmenopoulos indicates that the laws and stipulations recorded in the text might have continued to be relevant to urban planning in the Byzantine empire for centuries.[13]

In the study of Byzantine and Early Islamic Ascalon, Julian's text is best used not as a legal code per se but rather as a source of textual data, along the lines of the recovered material record, for interpreting the city of Ascalon. The most basic level of analysis for which the text can be used is to build a corpus of the city's architecture. The process of building a corpus of the city's architecture involves analysis of particular features, such as windows, doors, terraces, and sewage systems associated with those buildings. In discussing the features of various buildings it is possible to associate certain activities with many of the buildings because many of the structures are identified by their functions. As a corpus of material these buildings cease to be independent artifacts and become, rather, key features in the context of the built environment. These descriptions can be used for a second level of analysis that identifies patterns which not only illuminate aspects of the city plan and the continuing development of the city, but also lend greater meaning to the lists of buildings by providing them a context.

Julian of Ascalon organized his treatise according to the four elements, earth, wind, fire, and water, which he regarded as the source of all conflict between people. To make it more meaningful for archaeological research and the investigation of Ascalon, the text can be organized into buildings and/or activities that fall into the following categories: daily life, industry, service, commerce, residential, and infrastructure. Within each category buildings can be discussed in terms of characteristic features, location (within the city and in proximity to other structures), and function. The category of daily life, for instance, includes private bath houses and bakeries. In both cases Julian discusses hearths and/or fires as features of such buildings. The existence of hearths in these structures, or any nonresidential building for that matter, plays a large role in determining their location as does their proximity to neighboring buildings. The nature of nearby buildings, their height, placement of windows and doors, as well as the prevailing wind, further influence where a bath or bakery might be built.

The category of industry includes ceramic, gypsum and lime kilns, dyers, glassworks or factories, oil makers, rope makers, launderers, and finally *garum* and cheese makers. Again, as in the case of the bakeries and bath houses, these buildings are discussed in terms of their characteristic features and their locations within the city. Brothels, taverns, stables, and animal pens are included under the service heading. With the exception of brothels these buildings or activities are all allowed inside the city, although they are subject to rules that are designed, as in the case of industry, to minimize the nuisance posed to neighbors. Taverns, for example, are not allowed

---

13. Konstantinos Harmenopoulos, *Manuale legum sive hexabiblos: Cum appendicibus et legibus agrariis*, edited by Gustav Ernst Heimbach (Aalen, 1969).

to have benches outside their doors for fear that patrons might want to be served outside, thereby posing a nuisance to passersby. Julian offers less information about the features of these types of buildings, but their inclusion in his text further illustrates the variety of buildings to be found in Ascalon as well as their locations in all areas of the city.

The next category, commerce, includes warehouses and shops that are discussed not as aspects of formal institutions but rather as important features of various city neighborhoods. Warehouses, according to Julian, might be stand-alone structures or part of larger structures possibly wholly commercial in function or mixed-use buildings that combine commercial and residential space. Shops, often found along portico-lined streets, could also be found in mixed-use buildings with shops on the first floor and one or two upper floors of residences. In discussing shops, Julian addresses the issue of private shops extending their business into the porticoed walkways in front of them. Julian allows private shops to extend outward with the caveat that such activities must take place directly in front of a specific shop and may not extend sideways into the area of other shops.

The next category, residential structure, is of particular importance for interpreting Ascalon since it is the type of building for which we have the most direct archaeological evidence. The houses of sixth century Ascalon as described by Julian might be single story family homes or multistory, up to three or four stories high, condominium buildings. Residences could also be found in mixed-use buildings where in some cases residences and warehouses might even share a common courtyard. Julian mentions some of the common features of such buildings including courtyards, balconies, roof terraces, gutters, cisterns, and latrines in addition to the obvious windows and doors. Many of these features are identifiable in the archaeological record and information about those that are not is extremely valuable for better reconstructing entire structures.

The final category of infrastructure includes streets, porticos, public art, public gardens, and water and waste drainage and storage systems. Many of these aspects of the city are mentioned only within the context of Julian's discussions of specific buildings. It is nonetheless clear that they were important aspects of city life and that features such as public art and gardens were regarded as key mechanisms for ensuring that the city remained a pleasant community in which to reside. All together then the various categories of buildings, infrastructure, and activities found in Ascalon and presented in Julian's text provide a fairly detailed picture of sixth century Ascalon. Importantly, it is a picture that reflects the very aspects of the city also revealed in the archaeological record. The text complements the material culture record and provides a tool for not only reconstructing Ascalon in the sixth century but also for tracing how the city continued to develop into the Islamic period.

A starting point may be to take the buildings and infrastructure outlined in the categories just explored and situate them within the context of the city. This data can then be examined in light of the archaeological data and combined to create a more comprehensive context for the houses and their situation within the city. According to Julian's text, bath houses could be located anywhere within the city, including residential areas, so too could bakeries. Julian's text allows two important conclusions to be drawn. First, residential areas did not consist only of houses but also incorporated bakeries, baths, and other activities housed in stand-alone or multipurpose buildings. Secondly, important aspects of daily life such as food and hygiene were not limited to one area within the city but rather could be found in dispersed locations. Residents did not need to go to one specific area of the city to visit a bath or to buy some bread but could expect to find such services in their own neighborhoods.

As mentioned, the activities categorized in this study as industry are varied and include pottery kilns, gypsum/plaster kilns, lime kilns, dyers, glassworks and glass factories, oil makers, rope makers, fullers, and finally *garum* and cheese makers. Many of these industries were regarded as so dangerous or as presenting such a significant nuisance that they were relegated to spaces outside of the city. In some cases they were allowed within cities only if absolutely necessary and if such buildings were situated in the most isolated areas away from other buildings as much as possible. This information suggests that in the Byzantine period industry was, as much as possible, situated within more peripheral areas of the site where settlement might not have been as dense, thereby allowing industry to operate with minimum impact on neighbors. Julian's indication that activities traditionally situated outside the city could be moved inside if necessary might suggest that it was actually occurring, that buildings housing dangerous activities were being built in the city and that Julian was trying to regulate that process.

The rather general category of service includes brothels, taverns, and stables. Julian's writing clearly suggests the latter two activities or functions were to be found within the city, particularly along streets. In the case of brothels it is not clear whether such buildings could be found in Ascalon although archaeological evidence suggests that at one time Ascalon was home to at least one brothel.[14] The possibility remains that, while brothels were supposed to be located only in villages or rural areas, they might have been operating in towns. Julian's stipulations indicate certain activities should not be located in a town or that they should be in a particular part of town. To know how closely and for how long the regulations outlined in Julian's treatise were followed is not known.

In writing about commercial activities Julian indicates that warehouses could be independent buildings or space within a multipurpose building that might combine residential and other commercial spaces. The text leaves open the question of whether or not Ascalon might have had a warehouse district or specific commercial district. Shops figure prominently in discussions not only of streets, which they often lined, but also as ground floor occupants in mixed-use buildings. Julian's discussion of shops and warehouses indicates, much in the case of bakeries and baths, that they could be found in residential and nonresidential areas of the city. Warehouses and shops could be along major thoroughfares or smaller streets. Of particular note are the implications for how changes in the use of certain space is becoming more noticeable and, perhaps, more problematic. In his writing about shops and the use of space in the porticoed walkways in front of specific shops, Julian seems to indicate that encroachment or at the very least dealing with the relationship between private and public space was a growing concern in the mid-sixth century. It is equally clear that if this was a problem it was not limited to one area of the city but rather could be found anywhere that shops or other commercial establishments might be located.

Residential architecture and spaces figure prominently in Julian's treatise and a great deal can be learned about how they fit into the city based on his text. From Julian's discussion of various features of single family and multiunit buildings it is clear that multistory buildings and single story buildings, not to mention single family homes and condominium buildings, existed side by side, creating neighborhoods with diverse architecture. Houses could be located in densely settled neighborhoods or in areas where unused lots might also be found. Writing about city infrastructure, Julian records information about streets, public gardens and plantings, public

---

14. Excavation uncovered a bath house datable to the fourth century. Adjacent to that building was a large sewer in which the remains of more than one hundred infants were recovered. This discovery led archaeologists to conclude that the bath house may have been associated with a brothel and that unwanted babies were disposed of in the sewer. On this theory, see Stager, *Ashkelon Discovered*, p. 51.

art, and water and waste drainage and storage, indicating these aspects of the city were common
and well regulated. Julian's discussion of porticoed streets indicates that elements of the classical city were still very much alive and an important part of the city in the mid-sixth century. The
existence of public gardens indicates that, while Ascalon might have had a densely built urban
environment, that environment also included open spaces. This offers a possible explanation for
the extent of settlement found in the material record in which buildings were found on the
mounds and up against the city walls.

Julian's treatise describes a diverse, densely built urban environment that maximized the
available land within the city of Ascalon. It is clear that many areas or neighborhoods of the city
had buildings with different functions and it is difficult to discern, based on Julian's writing, a
strict separation of functions among various zones of the city. The city had diverse architecture
not only in its residential structures but also in its commercial and industrial facilities. Maintenance of public gardens and art were important, even though land was apparently at a premium,
and considered significant in ensuring that Ascalon was a pleasant city in which to reside. Finally, it is clear from Julian's text that villages or rural areas near Ascalon must have had various
industries or services not permitted in the city.

The material record of Ascalon collected over sixteen seasons of excavations not only illuminates some of the buildings and city infrastructure described by Julian but also provides
evidence for how the city continued to develop. On a general level it is possible to corroborate if
not absolutely confirm some important aspects of the city as described in the sixth century. Because excavation on the mounds and more interior areas of the city, presumably areas of dense
settlement, has produced little to no evidence of industrial or craft activity during the Byzantine
period, industry may have been relegated to more isolated areas of the city. At the beginning of
the Early Islamic period, the conversion of a former bath house into a kiln facility near Structure
Three indicates some change in the location of industry.

The area of Structure Three also provides evidence for the type of mixed neighborhood described by Julian, with the house first in the vicinity of a bath house and then a kiln. Even better
evidence comes from Structure One, which is a house located in proximity to a bath and a
church. The material record is clear: Ascalon had neighborhoods with both residential and nonresidential buildings in the Byzantine period and continued to do so in the Early Islamic period.
The lack of archaeological evidence for porticoed streets, shops, warehouses, and the types of
services described by Julian is best taken as a result of the random nature of excavation and not
as a refutation of the text. Better evidence exists for the residential architecture of Ascalon and
Julian's text does in fact render some of the architecture more meaningful. It is clear that the majority of houses are single family homes and that they can be found throughout the city. At least
one example appears to be a multifamily home, Structure Three, in which it is possible to identify courtyards perhaps associated with suites of rooms. The layout of the building is easily
interpreted as including multiple living units.

While the archaeological evidence of Ascalon reflects many of the patterns identified by
Julian, it also clearly shows the types of changes within the city that Julian may have been trying
to control or minimize. Excavation has uncovered dramatic changes in the function of some
buildings, culminating with the construction of a kiln during the Early Islamic period, in the vicinity of domestic structures. It is hard to know how extensive this pattern was throughout the
city but it undoubtedly marks a departure from the perceived ideal for city organization. Overall,
a strong sense of continuity remains in the architectural evidence and much that Julian writes
about Ascalon in the sixth century seems to be more or less accurate for the Early Islamic period.

The fact that the development of the city is marked by subtle rather then dramatic change is important for understanding, insofar as it is possible, the city's inhabitants.

One of the most striking aspects of the domestic architecture of Ascalon is the lack of evidence for the Islamic conquest; no evidence has been found that indicates the newly arrived inhabitants brought along new urban ideals that changed the cityscape of Ascalon. Whether this was because the existing city and its domestic structures were recognizable forms with which the inhabitants were comfortable, or because population pressures or the availability of building materials encouraged the utilization of existing structures, is unclear. The overall impression is simply one of continuity within the architecture and city plan of Ascalon. It would be misleading to argue that no evidence exists for change. The very maintenance and reuse of structures did result in some physical changes that can be traced through time. Certainly the ceramic corpus, which establishes the chronological framework for the city, shows change with the introduction of new ceramics and the disappearance of old forms. The nature of the corpus from Ascalon limits its usefulness for exact identifications and dating, however. This is because during the last century of settlement in medieval Ascalon the city repeatedly changed hands between Muslim and Crusader forces, with the result that the material record of Ascalon is highly disturbed, with few of the clean, sealed contexts archaeologists rely on for dating purposes. Although it is disturbed and devoid of any dramatic changes, the ceramic corpus of Ascalon does reflect a steady progression of ceramic types from Byzantine wares and early glazed wares to distinctive Middle Islamic glazed wares such as underglaze painted wares and incised wares.

The evidence from Ascalon, both archaeological and documentary, proves that using domestic architecture to interpret the city is an effective tool for analyzing urban development. It provides, moreover, insight to an important part of cities that is often overlooked: private rather than public architecture. In contrast to city centers or public architecture, which often reflect dramatic changes, the houses do not. They show, moreover, little evidence for political or military events, until the end of the city's settlement, leaving a mark on the city's residential areas. The evidence from Ascalon is surely repeated at other sites, with or without documentary material, where houses figure prominently in the archaeological record. Another ideal site at which to apply this methodology is Fustat, which has a well-published collection of domestic architecture and a readily available documentary resource, the Cairo Geniza. In fact, the relationship between text and archaeology is much clearer at Fustat than it is at Ascalon.

A number of scholars have studied the houses of Fustat, making contributions on a number of levels, ranging from discussions of construction materials and methods to more broad-ranging archaeological assessments. Shlomo D. Goitein's publication of contemporary textual evidence for the houses of Fustat provides archaeologists with a unique database and an invaluable interpretive tool for Fustat.[15] The documents of the Cairo Geniza act in much the same way Julian of Ascalon's treatise does; they serve as a source of raw data about the types of houses that might be found in Fustat and they provide a means to assess the city plan using those structures. The best sources of information on houses in the Cairo Geniza are deeds of purchase specifically and

---

15. Shlomo D. Goitein, "A Mansion in Fustat: A Twelfth-Century Description of a Domestic Compound in the Ancient Capital of Egypt," in *The Medieval City*, edited by Harry A. Miskimin, David Herlihy, and Abraham L. Udovitch (New Haven, 1977), pp. 163–78; idem, "Urban Housing in Fatimid and Ayyubid Times," *Studia Islamica* 47 (1978): 5–23. For the most complete discussion on houses and related topics by Goitein, see his *A Mediterranean Society: The Jewish Communities of the Arab World as Portrayed in the Documents of the Cairo Geniza* (Berkeley, 1983), and refer to Volume 4: *Daily Life*, pp. 47–150.

legal documents more generally. Such documents usually include information on the location of the property, its name, its characteristic parts, boundaries, details about proprietors and proprietorship, price, and any special conditions associated with the property. Although Goitein does not identify constituent elements for an identifiable basic house form, he identifies a typology of three house forms using descriptions of domestic architecture in the Cairo Geniza that can be applied to the structures excavated by Bahgat and Gabriel and Scanlon.

Goitein labels the first house type the "bazaar house."[16] This type of house consists of stores or commercial space on a ground floor that is topped by one or two upper floors of residences. In this type of structure separate entrances for the shops or commercial space and the residences are common. It is difficult to identify this type of building because preservation at most sites is limited to ground floor wall levels and nowhere is this truer than at Fustat.[17] Maison VI and Groupe I have ground floor plans that suggest they might be examples of Goitein's "bazaar house." The most striking example, Groupe I, identified as a single building, displays a complexity in form, layout, and possibly function that is not found in any of the other structures excavated by Bahgat and Gabriel (fig. 2.11).[18] The structure, which is bounded on three sides by streets, includes a number of distinctive functional areas that are easily discerned in its organization. Two primary means of access into Groupe I are found on the north side of the structure. The first is a doorway leading from the street into a vestibule that provides access to a house with all the requisite features identified by Bahgat and Gabriel, the focal point of which is Cour C. A second courtyard, Cour D, is surrounded by a suite of rooms; the exact function of this unit, whether it is part of the Cour C unit or an entirely separate unit, is unclear.

Just to the east of the doorway leading into the Cour C house is an alley labeled impasse that provides access to two other areas within Groupe I. At the south end of the alley a doorway leads into a vestibule from which two distinct houses, one oriented around Cour B and a second oriented around Cour A, can be accessed. Again, both of these units have the requisite features identified as key elements of houses in Fustat. At a minimum three residences, possibly four, can be identified within Groupe I, but the additional spaces within this building allow it to be characterized as an example of the "bazaar house." Back in the alley a doorway on the east side provides access to a colonnaded room that has a distinctive layout unlike those found in the residential units. Missing in this space is a central courtyard, an *iwan*, or even a hall, suggesting this space did not function as a house. The layout certainly does not fit the model of the "central-courtyard house" developed by Bahgat and Gabriel. An explanation for this space might be that it was nonresidential space attached to the house. It could have been commercial or craft space for the home's owner. Even better evidence for commercial space in Groupe 1 comes from the north side of the building where evidence of two shops is found along the street. These one-room shops are clearly part of the larger structure and indicate that Groupe I was probably a mixed use building with both residential and commercial space. In the absence of published material culture or any interpretive discussion of this structure by the excavators, any conclusion about its exact function must remain hypothetical. When the evidence is examined in the context of documents from the Cairo Geniza, however, a direct correlation seems to exist between Goitein's "bazaar house" and the layout and function of Groupe I.

---

16. On house types, see Goitein, "Urban Housing in Fatimid and Ayyubid Times," pp. 14–15.

17. Some exceptions include a number of sites in Egypt, such as Karanis, where evidence for upper stories is found in the material record.

18. Ali Bahgat and Albert Gabriel, *Fouilles d'al Fustat, publiées les auspices du Comité de conservation des monuments de l'art arabe* (Paris, 1921); Albert Gabriel, *Les fouilles d'al Foustat et les origines de la maison arabe en Égypte* (Paris, 1921).

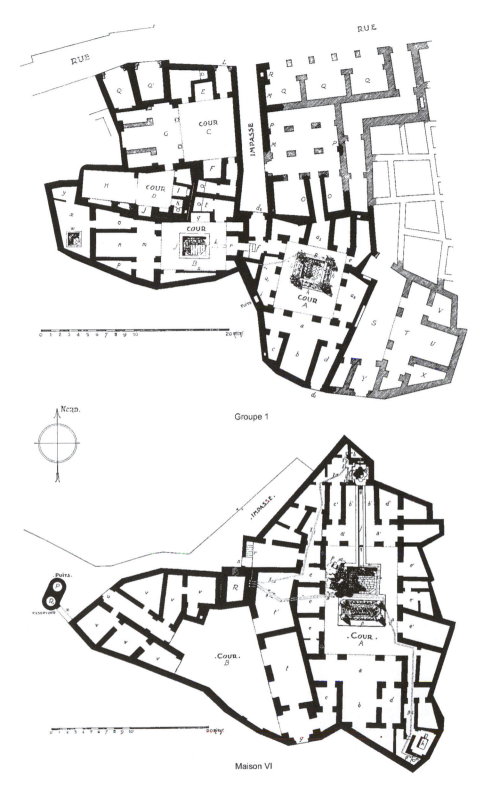

Figure 2.11. "Bazaar house": Fustat groupe I and maison VI. Fustat
(after Bahgat and Gabriel, *Fouilles d'al Fustat*)

According to Goitein, the most frequently mentioned type of house in the Geniza documents is the "family house." This type of house might be a single structure or a compound containing several structures belonging to one family. Based on information about such houses Goitein was able to produce a schematic plan of a standard "family house" that is remarkably similar to some of the houses actually uncovered during the excavation of Fustat.[19] Of the eight houses published by Bahgat and Gabriel at least three, Maisons III, IV, and VII, appear to correspond to this type (fig. 2.12). The first example, Maison III, is an individual structure organized around a central courtyard. This courtyard, which has a pool and fountain construction similar to that found in Maison VI, is the focal point of the structure and is surrounded by rooms on all four sides. Access into the structure is provided by two entrances, both of which pass through either a hallway or a vestibule before leading into the courtyard.[20]

The organization of Maison III clearly fits the "family house" model identified by Goitein. So too does Maison IV, which is also a solitary structure organized around a courtyard with rooms on two sides. This house also has two entrances, both from the same street on the north side of the building, that provide access into the interior of the house through long hallways. The parallels between these houses that have courtyards with pools or fountains that serve as a focal point, suites of rooms around the courtyards, and multiple entrances are notable. While Maison VII also fits the "family house" model, some distinctions exist between it and the previous two. First, it is not a stand-alone house but rather appears to share a common wall with at least one neighboring house. Maison VII does have a central courtyard, with rooms on all four sides, but does not have a fountain or pool. In addition, the house has only one entrance, which leads from the street into a small vestibule that provides access to the courtyard. The range of forms and organization of these houses, within which both similarities and distinctions are visible, reflects the variety of descriptions for such structures in the Geniza documents.

The third house type identified by Goitein is the "apartment house." This type consists of a building three or more stories high. According to Goitein, evidence for this type of house comes from terms such as "middle and upper floors" used to describe such houses. No obvious examples of this type of structure were found at Fustat, in large part because preservation at the site does not allow for the identification of upper floors. It is necessary to look for this type of house in the available ground plans; one structure might be an example of a multiunit building if not an "apartment house." The building in question is Maison II, in which the basic plan appears to include two distinct living units (fig. 2.13). The building is accessed by a single entrance from the street that leads into a large room or enclosure rather than a vestibule. From that room three doorways open into different areas of the structure. To the north (room g) passing through a series of small rooms or halls, access is gained to Cour B, which is surrounded on three sides by rooms. The organization of this part of Maison II has all the basic elements of a house as defined by Bahgat and Gabriel: courtyard, hall, and *iwan*.

Back in the enclosure, on the west side a doorway opens to a short flight of stairs providing access to a hallway (o) which in turn provides access to Cour A which has rooms on at least two sides. This area of Maison II also has the requisite elements that allow it to be identified as a house and it seems possible that in this structure are two living units for two families. This interpretation is somewhat strengthened by a more careful comparison between the actual and

---

19. Goitein, "A Mansion in Fustat," p. 165.

20. One interesting feature of this house not found in
      others is a garden that Bahgat and Gabriel identified
      on its northeastern side.

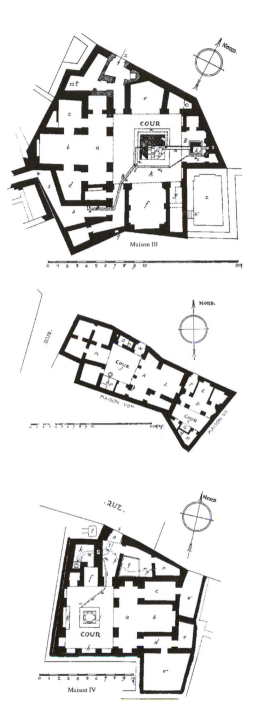

Figure 2.12. "Family house": Maison III, IV, VII, and VIIbis. Fustat
(after Bahgat and Gabriel, *Fouilles d'al Fustat*)

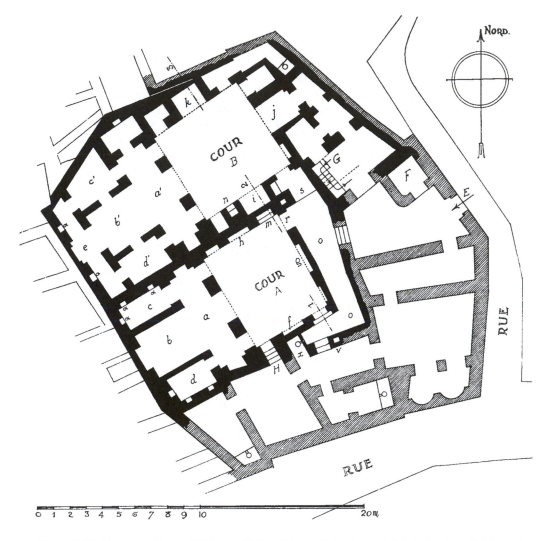

Figure 2.13. "Apartment house": Maison II. Fustat (after Bahgat and Gabriel, *Fouilles d'al Fustat*)

reconstructed architectural plans provided by Bahgat and Gabriel. On the reconstructed plan a doorway (s) connects the two courtyards linking the two apparent housing units into one complex. On the actual plan, however, a wall in place of the doorway may suggest that the two areas were not directly connected and that they might be two housing units within one structure. Maison II could include two housing units, which makes it identifiable as a possible example of an "apartment house" or multiunit building.

Goitein labels the fourth type of house a "multistoried house," of which only one example is mentioned in the Geniza documents. This house has a ground floor and nine upper stories. Goitein is hesitant to identify it as an actual house type and with good reason. The word used for story, *tabaqa*, is also used to refer to an apartment forming part of a story. It is possible, therefore, that this house with nine stories is simply a house that has nine upper apartments on an undisclosed number of stories. As mentioned in the discussion of apartment houses and how they might be identified, the quality of preservation in Fustat does not allow for the identification of this type of house in the material record.[21]

The range of forms identified in Goitein's typology includes single and multifamily homes as well as buildings that combined commercial and residential space.[22] From information in Geniza documents, these buildings were found side by side in neighborhoods with diversified architecture and organization. Both these patterns echo descriptions of the houses and city plan of Ascalon as described by Julian of Ascalon in the mid-sixth century. That similarity raises some interesting questions, one of the most intriguing of which is whether or not structures combining commercial and residential space can or should be interpreted as insula. Goitein addresses this question in an article on urban housing in Fatimid and Ayyubid times acknowledging that Ahmad Fakhri, an Egyptian archaeologist, "... categorically denied that insulae existed in Egypt."[23] That denial rings false in light of the "bazaar house" type identified by Goitein and suggests that some reassessment is necessary.

Any resolution on the existence of insula in cities such as Fustat or Ascalon is beyond the scope of this paper, but such discussions demonstrate the potential for examining houses not only as individual structures, but also as important facets of the built environment that contribute to the study of cities as much as studies of institutions or city centers. In addition, the study of houses at these sites provides an important tool for examining social identity, to see how inhabitants are reflected in the domestic architecture of a city. At Ascalon it is possible to show that whatever the makeup of the population in the Early Islamic period, the inhabitants lived in and used as much of the city as had the population in the Byzantine period. In the case of Fustat, the evidence indicates that diverse inhabitants lived in the same type of housing, and architecturally little distinguishes between houses built and lived in by Jews, Muslims, or Copts. Of course, the addition of other types of material culture can make the identification of a house's inhabitants a little clearer, but even ceramics with an Arabic inscription or a cross cannot be regarded as proof positive for the religious identity of those residing in the house.

Towards an understanding of cities in the Byzantine and Early Islamic periods, the analysis of non-public areas can provide a valuable counterpoint to the study of a city center. As the function of public buildings change, and as houses are built on what were once thoroughfares, signs of dramatic change are left behind. By examining public and non-public areas together it should be possible to elaborate a more nuanced analysis of a city's evolution/growth. The development of archaeological applications for documentary evidence, such as Julian of Ascalon's text and even the mosaic depictions of Ascalon, further expands the potential for utilizing diverse databases to explore many aspects of cities, their architecture, and how they evolved during the medieval period.

---

21. Whether or not such buildings existed in Fustat is a question of some interest. At least one medieval source does describe houses five and six stories tall (Khusraw, *Book of Travels*, pp. 59–61).

22. Readily identifiable in the material excavated by Bahgat and Gabriel, the same typology of houses can be applied to Scanlon's later excavations. In the case of this material, however, the identifications of specific housing forms is more challenging due to the preservation of the structures uncovered by Scanlon.

23. See Goitein, "Urban Housing in Fatimid and Ayyubid Times," p. 15.

3

SAMARQAND IN THE EIGHTH CENTURY: THE EVIDENCE OF TRANSFORMATION

YURY KAREV

Russian Academy of Sciences, Institute of World History, Moscow
French-Uzbek archaeological Mission in Samarqand

The spread of Islam proceeded differently in different areas; the intensive internal evolution of the Muslim community meant that this process varied greatly at different periods of time. The status of the non-Muslim country to be conquered was particularly important. Besides the religious motivation — affirming the new vision of the universe — two major factors determined the political approach of the caliphate rulers to expansion from the seventh to eighth centuries. First was the wealth of the population and the economic interest it represented, and second, the dominant cult in the region. The position towards pagan religions was certainly most severe and used to justify, in case of military resistance, the holy war (*ghazw*) "without mercy," carried out until the enemy was totally defeated. At the same time, destruction from war was not extended blindly for the simple reason that the old infrastructure was, at least in the beginning, indispensable for establishing control over the local population and collecting taxes. Only pagan temples, idols, and sacred books were in some cases, but not always, deliberately destroyed and burned in order to proclaim the ultimate goal of the mission. Despite the resulting shock brought by the collapse of the old religions, the local population was involved in the long process of integration into the new state system and the formation of a unified, if very varied, world.

During the sixth to seventh centuries, the countries of the Māwarā'annahr (Transoxiana) were extremely rich and utterly pagan (exception made for the Christian and Jewish communities). Besides that, they were in permanent rivalry with one another. The geopolitical position of Samarqand, the capital of Sughd, the core region of the Māwarā'annahr, determined the particularities of the culture of the country. The two main cultural influences came, on the one hand, from China, and on the other, from Iran. But the importance of the Turkic political power in the region in the seventh to eighth centuries should not be neglected. Samarqand, like some other urban centers in Māwarā'annahr, played a crucial role in international trading between East and West. An important part of the benefits accruing to the city was the creation of conditions for the prosperity of the people, and as a result, the intensive development of all sorts of arts and crafts ranging from decorative mural paintings to objects for domestic use. A distinctive Sogdian style of art was elaborated before Islam that included different local and transformed foreign elements.

One of the most significant impacts on the local history of Samarqand is due to the Arab invasion. The multiple episodes of military campaigns in Khurāsān and Māwarā'annahr from the end of the seventh to the first half of the eighth century in chronicles like *Ta'rīkh ar-rusul wa-l-mulūk* of aṭ-Ṭabarī are not only very detailed but occupy a major place in the author's year-by-year description of the history of the caliphate. This is due, obviously, to the predominant role of the oriental direction in the external policy of the Umayyad state at that time. There is no room here for detailing the historical description, but one point should be elaborated on: during the eighth century (particularly between 705 and 752) the struggles between two communities were extremely severe. All the campaigns of Arab commanders like Qutayba b. Muslim or Saʿīd b. ʿAmr al-Ḥarashī, and later Abū Muslim, were characterized by the persecution of the rebellious Sogdian leaders, the *dihqan*s (*dahāqīn*) and their kings, and were accompanied by heavy casualties, especially on the other side. Nevertheless, the resistance of the local rulers, with some exceptions, was extremely persistent. In reality there was a long process of imposed redistribution of wealth.

As an example, consider the following lines from a Middle Persian poem lamenting the Arab conquest:

> 5   "With one blow that band (of Arabs) has enfeebled our religion and killed the princes. We are laid low and they <lord it over us> like devils."
>
> 7   "By force they have taken men's wives from them, their private property, their orchards and gardens.
>
> 8   They have imposed the poll tax and apportioned it upon our heads. They have demanded the basic rent and a heavy impost as well."
>
> 12   "Lo, we shall pull down their mosques and set up again the sacred fires ..."[1]

An independent view of the situation held by opponents of the Muslims is preserved in very few non-Christian sources. Whatever the period of this poem and the region of its composition, we can use it in order to illustrate how the Iranian-speaking population from Ctesiphon to Samarqand perceived the Arab conquerors. Fortunately, the Chinese chronicles have preserved some letters from the local rulers to the T'ang Emperor, all of them composed in similar terms.[2]

Samarqand was taken in 712 by Qutayba b. Muslim after a long siege and many fierce battles. A treaty was concluded between the Arab general and *ikhshīd* Ghūrak, the king of Sughd, involving an immense sum in the way of contributions. The occupation of a part of the city by the Arabs was not included in the treaty, but at the last moment Qutayba changed his mind and forced the *ikhshīd* to leave the capital. Ghūrak chose Ishtikhan, situated northwest of Samarqand, as his residence.

Following these events, Samarqand enters a new period of its history. One of the most important problems for archaeologists consists in knowing what kind of material remains exist on the site from the époque and what archaeological evidence could (or could not) reflect the changing population and its interactions. The best place to carry out this study would presumably be in the zone protected by the citadel of the city, the seat of the new power in a hostile environment.

The first Arab building in the city, according to the sources, was the mosque erected by Qutayba b. Muslim on the site of the fire-temple immediately after the capture of Samarqand in 712. "Samarkand was a place of pilgrimage (*ḥaǧǧ*) for the heathens, the Friday mosque that is now in Samarkand was a heathen place of worship (*muʿbad*) and a temple of idols (*butkhāna*) in ancient times."[3] Qutayba has ordered gathering the idols together and despoiling them. An enormous pile of idols ("like a *qaṣr*" castle) was set on fire by Qutayba's own hand.[4] The sense

1. François de Blois, "A Persian Poem Lamenting the Arab Conquest," in *Studies in Honour of Clifford Edmund Bosworth*, Volume 2: *The Sultan's Turret: Studies in Persian and Turkish Culture*, edited by Carole Hillenbrand (Leiden, 2000), p. 92.

2. Edouard Chavannes, editor, *Documents sur les Tou-Kiue (Turcs) occidentaux* (Recueillis et commentés suivi de notes additionnelles par Edouard Chavannes; Paris, 1904), pp. 203–05.

3. Vasilij Bartol'd, *Turkestan v epoxu mongol'skago nashestvija*, Volume 1: *Texty* (St. Peterburg, 1898), p. 49.

4. Abū Jaʿfar Muḥammad b. Jarīr aṭ-Ṭabarī, *Taʾrīkh ar-rusul wa-l-mulūk*, Volume 2, p. 1246; Aḥmad b. Yaḥya al-Balādhurī, *Kitāb futūḥ al-buldān*, p. 421.

of this act was obvious — a humiliation of the pagan idol cults and a manifestation of the power of Islam.

Frantz Grenet, referring to the plan of the temples in Penjikent, supposes that this act took place in the large courtyard in front of the temple.[5] The problem is that the excavation in this zone has still not yielded any architectural remains that could be interpreted with confidence as those of a temple or an early mosque. There is nevertheless a part of an edifice with a corner tower that could be the remains of a temple (see below). In any case, for the first mosque, we cannot be sure whether it was a new building deliberately constructed on the destroyed temple or a fire-temple transformed into this mosque.

The works of local history, the *Kitāb al-Qand* and Persian *Qandiya*, mention at least two other mosques in the city constructed by the *'ulamā'* who came along with Qutayba, Muḥammad b. Wāsiʿ and aḍ-Ḍaḥḥak b. Muzāḥim. As in the case of the Friday mosque of Qutayba we have no idea about their plan or architectural style. According to aṭ-Ṭabarī, a part of the population, in response to the call of the Khurāsān's governor al-Ashras b. ʿAbd Allāh in A.H. 110/728–729 C.E., started to convert to Islam and to construct the mosques.[6]

We know also that one group of the learned men (*'ulamā'*) was charged by Qutayba with determining the correct orientation of Samarqand towards Mecca (*qibla* direction) in order to build the *miḥrāb*s (*maḥārib*) of the Friday mosque as well as of the other mosques in the city. In other words, a special commission was organized, including the most authoritative *'ulamā'* who came with the Arab army and whose names were preserved in *Kitāb al-Qand*.[7]

So, on the one hand we have these clear indications of the construction activity of the Muslims in Samarqand, and on the other the great scarcity of archaeological data from the first part of the eighth century. During the 720s and 730s the Arabs were constantly threatened by the revolts and riots of the Sogdians and by the incursions of the Turks. Once, around 734–735, they probably lost the city for a while. Thus, the general situation did not stimulate the colonists to build much. At the same time, the Sogdians were not ready to adopt the innovations brought by the Muslims since their force of resistance was not completely exhausted.

On the other hand, with the installation of the new colonists in the conquered area the process of integration was under way. Many Sogdians became the *mawlā*s (*mawālī*) of the members of different Arab tribes and participated in military operations with the Arab commanders. As everywhere in the conquered countries the process of Islamization was much more intensive in urban centers than in rural areas. The Arabs brought and established new political institutions, which found their expression in new forms of architecture. This last statement is based on the results of our excavations in Samarqand during the last twelve years.

NEW ARCHAEOLOGICAL DATA

This archaeological expedition was organized by Paul Bernard, Frantz Grenet, and Muxammadzhon Isamiddinov and began work at Afrasiab, the ancient Samarqand, in 1989. Many archaeological elements have been discovered from the Islamic period, dated between the

5. Xasan Axunbabaev and Frantz Grenet, "La mosquée cathédrale: Fouilles de la mission franco-soviètique à l'ancienne Samarkand (Afrasiab): Première campagne, 1989, par MM Paul Bernard, Frantz Grenet, Muxammedzon Isamiddinov et leurs collaborateurs," *Comptes Rendus de l'Académie des Inscriptions et Belles-Lettres* (Paris, 1990): 370.

6. Aṭ-Ṭabarī, *Ta 'rīkh*, p. 1508.

7. Naǧm ad-Dīn ʿUmar b. Muḥammad an-Nasafī, *al-Qand fī dhikr 'ulamā' Samarqand*, edited by Yūsuf al-Hādī (Tehran 1999), pp. 178–79, 603.

eighth and the thirteenth century, when the city was destroyed by Genghis Khan's troops. This research builds upon over a century of field research by successive Russian and Soviet expeditions to this famous site. Since 1991 the author has been co-director with his Uzbek colleague Dr. A. Atakhodjaev of the excavations on the lower terrace of the citadel of Samarqand. From the year 2000 up until this latest season in 2002, the ongoing research on the site has been made possible thanks to the Max Van Berchem Foundation.

The site of Afrasiab occupied an area of almost 220 ha from the moment of its foundation in the sixth century B.C. (fig. 3.1). The core of the site is situated in the north and formed by the citadel and the so-called sacred area where the main religious buildings were situated (as far as we can infer from the remains of the mosques of the eighth and thirteenth centuries; fig. 3.2). It is here, in the northern part of the site, that most of the archaeological activities of the mission have taken place.

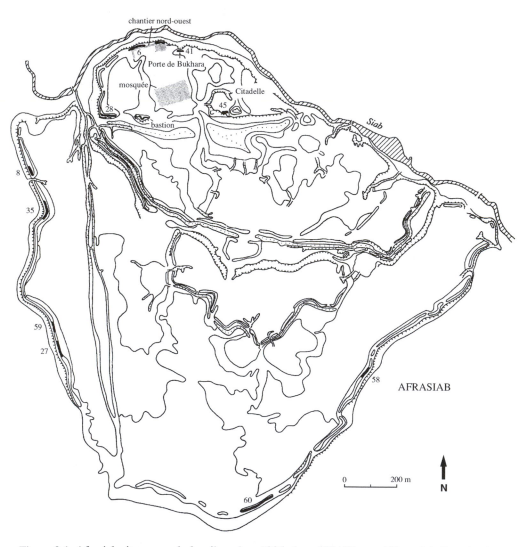

Figure 3.1. Afrasiab site, general plan (based on 1885 plan of Vasiliev and Kuzmin). Drawing by G. Lecuyot, "Fouilles de la mission franco-soviètique à l'ancienne Samarkand," *Comptes Rendus de l'Académie des Inscriptions et Belles-Lettres* (Paris, 1990): 357

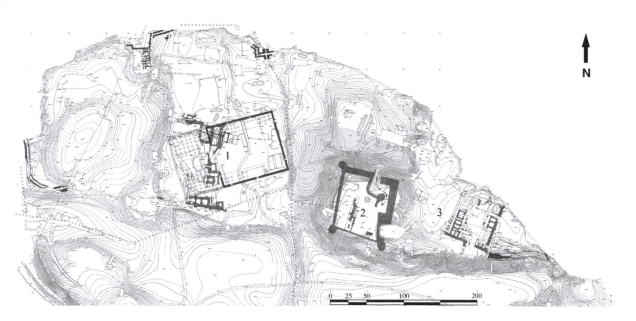

Figure 3.2. Northern part of the Afrasiab site. (1) "Sacred area" with the complex of the eighth century and mosques above it, (2) citadel-donjon, and (3) lower terrace of the citadel with the *dār al-imāra* from the middle of the eighth century (Franco-Uzbek archaeological mission in Samarqand; different plans unified by Cl. Rapin)

The first important architectural remains that we could relate to the Arab construction activities in the city have been found in this "sacred area" (fig. 3.2: Area 1). Despite what could have been expected, the building discovered can hardly be interpreted as a mosque. The huge complex being excavated by Frantz Grenet and Igor Ivanickij in the mosque area of Afrasiab belongs to the new type of architecture and indicates some important changes in its planning (fig. 3.3).[8] First of all, its plan is possibly organized around a central courtyard (ca. 50 × 45 m) although only the part to the east was excavated and remains of the building were badly damaged both in ancient times and by the excavators at the beginning of the twentieth century. The complex is oriented on cardinal points; its size is about 115 × 84 m. External walls are more than 4 m wide, strengthened by massive half-towers and corner towers. All the walls of the building were erected using the same technique— two courses of mudbricks (50 × 31 × 14 cm) were placed between two courses of pisé. This technique fits comfortably with the Sogdian tradition.

The complex certainly had two distinctive parts, opposite one another, on the north and the south. The part to the south is much more comprehensible from an architectural point of view. A distinctive unit, which can be called a *bayt*, with a separate disposition was enhanced by a probable axial corridor from the west and by two perpendicular corridors from the north and east. The unit itself was organized around a central courtyard or hall of about 19 × 11 m. All the rooms of varying interior dimensions were paved, probably in the second period, by thick burned

---

8. The description of the complex is based on the article published in Russian: Franc Grene [Frantz Grenet] and Igor Ivanickij, "Dvorec omeyadskogo namestnika pod mechet'ju abbasidskogo perioda na Afrasiabe," in *Arxeologija, numizmatika i épigrafika srednevekovoj Srednej Azii, Materialy nauchnoj konferencii, posvjashchennoj 60-letiju so dnja rozhdenija d.i.n. B.D. Kochneva (15. XII. 2000)* (Samarqand, 2000), pp. 58–62. I would like to express my gratitude to Frantz Grenet for his permission to publish the most recent field plan of the complex (fig. 3.3).

bricks ($44 \times 38 \times 6$ cm), which are in fact the earliest example of large-scale brick production of this type. The Sogdians usually used mudbricks and pisé (*pakhsa*), with the exception of some special constructions requiring burned bricks, such as bathrooms. The baked bricks have preserved rectangular stamps with Arabic inscriptions, probably the marks of the manufacturer; for the most part these are not deciphered with confidence. In 1904 Vasili Barthold saw bricks with the inscriptions "*ikhshīd*" and "Ishtikhan," the name of the city situated to the northeast of Samarqand, where the *ikhshīd*s were compelled to move after 712. The proposed reading is still hypothetical and inspires polemics. The most distinctive unit in the northern half of the complex is the rectangular room, 20.0×11.5 m, the proportions of which are very close to that of the reception halls of Sogdian architecture. The ceramics in the rubble layer inside the rooms can be dated from the end of the eighth century to the beginning of the ninth and belong to the third and last period of occupation of the complex. The *terminus ante quem non* is defined by the finding in the east wall of a coin of Turghar (738 to ca. 750 C.E.), the last king, an *ikhshīd* of Sughd who had the prerogative to mint his own coinage.

The interpretation of this building is complicated by two problems. Apart from the fact that the "sacred area" is very badly damaged and extremely difficult to excavate, the complex has been excavated only partially and its known parts seem not to have been erected at the same time. The plan looks like a block of different composite units protected and reinforced by a massive external enclosure. The presence of the walls and towers built on almost the same level on opposite sides of the huge area is, indeed, the principal criterion for the interpretation of these architectural elements as a unified complex. On the one hand, the plan and the size of the complex apparently do not belong to the local tradition, to judge by its latest stage from the samples from Afrasiab itself and other archaeological sites in Sughd (see below). At the same time, the construction techniques mentioned above, the ramp leading to the second floor in the south bay, and particularly the lack of symmetry, as well as evident irregularity of the general setting and plausible use of previous constructions, all reflect the transitional period between two traditions. In the archaeologist's opinion, the building, probably the first administrative palace, was constructed by the governor of Khurāsān Naṣr b. Sayyār (738–748) in the 740s, who succeeded in making peace with the Sogdians and calming the situation for some years.

It is important to note that the orientation of the complex follows the general disposition in the previous periods of walls in the "sacred area." A mosque built after 770 shows clear evidence that the *qibla* direction was different (fig. 3.3), even though the northern part of its complex has completely disappeared under the later mosque of the early thirteenth century. The southern part was certainly leveled at the beginning of the ninth century, when the mosque was enlarged to the west.

The question remains on the situation of the first mosque of Qutayba. One may expect its orientation towards *qibla* should be the same as with the later mosques. As we know from other examples, the mosque could be included in the palatial building (Qaṣr al-Ḥayr ash-Sharqī, Khirbat al-Minya, Ukhayḍīr among others), but in the case of the public Friday mosque the latter was usually erected outside of the *dār al-imāra*, being nevertheless placed close to it (al-Kūfa, ʿAnǧar, and so forth).

It should be remembered that in the old cities in general and much more in the fortified zones like a citadel space was always limited, even if the previous buildings had been leveled. In ʿAmmān, for instance, the mosque (the orientation of which is different than that of the rest of the edifices) was built in the center of the "L"-shaped citadel hill, where the space allowed a most convenient disposition outside the *dār al-imāra* limited by the external walls of the narrow

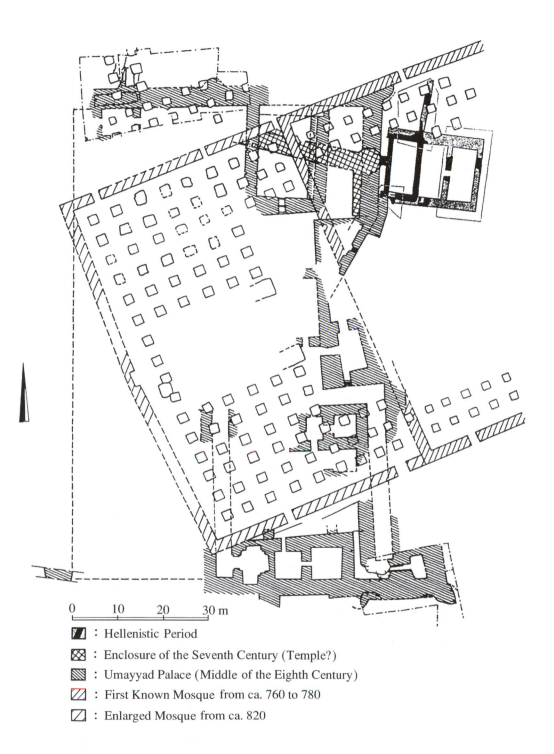

0   10   20   30 m

▨ : Hellenistic Period

⊠ : Enclosure of the Seventh Century (Temple?)

▨ : Umayyad Palace (Middle of the Eighth Century)

▨ : First Known Mosque from ca. 760 to 780

▱ : Enlarged Mosque from ca. 820

Figure 3.3. Different structures on the "sacred area." Afrasiab

northern part.[9] Thus, economy of space should play an important role. In other words, a new building could be constructed by the Muslims with the same orientation as the with the ancient one, an exception being when the mosque was included as an irregular element in the new structure. If this was the case in Samarqand, the first mosque, of a relatively small size, could be constructed close to the eastern side of the palace, as already suggested by Frantz Grenet. Nevertheless, the zone to the north and northeast of the plateau should not be entirely excluded (fig. 3.2: north of Area 1). In any case, the archaeological data shows the Arabs started to construct new buildings and change the situation in Samarqand.

Usually the royal palaces were constructed near to the donjon (called *keshk*), on the lower terrace; that is precisely the case of the building discovered and excavated since 1991.[10] The citadel at Samarqand can be divided into two parts: the donjon situated on the highest point of the site (fig. 3.2) and a lower area to the east of this castle (fig. 3.2: Area 3). This type of structure, with a "two-part citadel," is well known from other sites in Central Asia such as Pendjikent. The plan of this complex represents an important phase in the architectural history of the region. It consists of two different parts (figs. 3.4–5). The first, major one is a rectangular structure 65 × 55 m, organized around an inner central court. The second part includes a relatively narrow oblong court, located between the western wall of the palace itself (wall of the western row of rooms), and another external wall, situated 17 m westwards. The use of massive octagonal columns (2 m diameter) in both courts appears to be one of the most distinctive features of the monument.

In the first case, an arched gallery surrounded (on all four sides) an interior courtyard around which all rooms of the eastern part of the building were grouped. In the second case, the columns were initially planned to support a covered arched gallery built in front of the western wall of the building along the side of the "exterior" courtyard space, opposite the donjon. The colonnade of the outer courtyard also had two half-pillars — the pilaster attached to the southern wall, which was excavated, and by deduction a symmetrical one against the northern wall. The building had three towers on the eastern side, two in the corners and one in the center (fig. 3.5). Each tower is 3.5 m in diameter, a size which indicates that they served a decorative rather than a defensive function. The walls were built in seven or eight courses of mudbricks (47 × 23 × 7–8 cm) alternating with blocks of pisé (200 × 86 × 80 cm). The main gate was situated on the south side opposite the *iwān* on the north side of the palace. Two massive pillars (3.5 m large each) formed an impressive portal 5 m wide outside the building and about 11 m deep. On the west side two symmetrically disposed narrow corridors gave access to the main building (fig. 3.5).

According to the archaeological evidence, the whole area was leveled (the buildings from previous periods were almost completely destroyed) and the surface prepared for the construction of a new building. It is thus possible to conclude that a radical reorganization of the architectural space of the citadel took place in the middle of the eighth century. The building itself was designed with such precision that it was possible to reconstitute the unexcavated parts by simply applying the principles of axial symmetry. The fact that this enormous new building should have occupied the greater part of the lower half of the citadel clearly reflects its dominant function.

9. Antonio Almagro, "El Alcázar Omeya de Ammán," in *El esplendor de los Omeyas Cordobeses, la civilización musulmana de Europa Occidental: Exposición en Madinat al-Zahra, 3 de mayo a 30 de septiembre de 2001*, edited by Junta de Andalucía (Granada, 2001), p. 50.

10. Yury Karev, "Un palais islamique du VIIIe siècle à Samarkand," *Studia Iranica* 29 (2000): 273–96. For the most recent data, see idem, "Nouvelles recherches dans la citadelle de l'ancienne Samarkand," *Bulletin de la Fondation Max van Berchem* 15 (2001): 1–4.

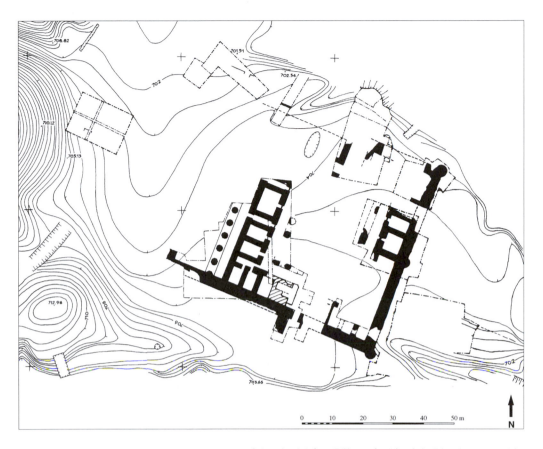

Figure 3.4. *Dār al-imāra* on the lower terrace of the citadel (ca. 750 C.E.). Afrasiab. Plan by E. Kurkina

There can be no doubt that it was built on the citadel of the city in order to house the administrative and political apparatus of the caliph's representative and should therefore be identified as the governor's palace, the *dār al-imāra*.

This palace was never finished according to its initial plan since there is no evidence of intensive occupation of the building during this first phase. Indeed, no remains of stucco or wall paintings have been found, yet it is logical to suppose that elements of architectural decoration such as these would have existed in a building of this type. Clearly some event must have disrupted the execution of the initial plans of the architect and led to the construction work coming to a halt. The first phase of construction can be dated, thanks to monetary finds in the foundation level under the walls (the coin of Turghar, *ikhshīd* of Sughd), from the 740s to the 750s.

After a while, the authorities that were ruling the city decided to finish the building with the means available at that time. These means were clearly not comparable to those of their predecessors, either financially or intellectually, and led to a considerable simplification of the initial plan; it is during this constructive phase that baked bricks were used for the first time, both in the masonry of the walls enclosing the outer and inner colonnades and in the paving of many rooms. This second period of construction, separated from the first by a short interval, can be dated between the second half of the 750s and the 770s (thanks to the first coins of Abū Muslim from Samarqand — beginning of the 750s, at those minted by al-Ashʿath b. Yaḥyā [A.H. 144/760–761 C.E.] and al-Ǧunayd b. Khālid at Bukhara [A.H. 151/768 C.E.]). The third period can be

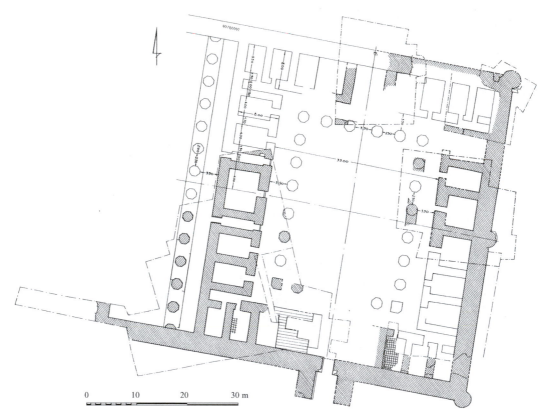

Figure 3.5. *Dār al-imāra* on the lower terrace of the citadel (ca. 750 C.E.). Afrasiab.
Plan and reconstruction by E. Kurkina

dated to the end of the eighth and the first half of the ninth century (by "black *dirhams*," with the name of the caliph al-Amīn (A.H. 193–198/809–813 C.E.). Finally, we date the fourth period to the middle of the ninth century, in other words to the beginning of the Samanid period. The scope of these modifications enables us to suppose that the building survived in a progressively more and more distorted form up until the tenth century.

HISTORICAL CONTEXT

Archaeological excavations are particularly important because of the silence of the historical sources about so many aspects of the history of the area. In this context, the discovery of a building such as a great palace or temple is all the more helpful. The size and the type of plan used for such structures can be precious witnesses of politically significant events that are not described in historical sources or only mentioned in cursory fashion. The complete analysis of the sources was made in a special article on the matter;[11] the following text presents the essential conclusions.

With all necessary precautions, the newly discovered administrative complex in Samarqand can be interpreted as a creation of the leader of the 'Abbasid movement Abū Muslim. He had an

---

11. Yury Karev, "La politique d'Abū Muslim dans le Māwarā'annahr: Les nouvelles données textuelles et archéologiques," *Der Islam* 79 (2002): 1–46.

obvious predilection for construction activity. Various Arab and Persian sources mention the remarkable buildings erected on the order of Abū Muslim in at least three major cities of Khurāsān: a *dār al-imāra* and a new congregational mosque in Marw, a mosque in Nīshāpūr, and a huge wall in Samarqand. A number of Arab authors (aṭ-Ṭabarī, al-Maqdīsī, an-Nasafī, Ibn al-Athīr) say that Abū Muslim built the wall of Samarqand in A.H. 134/751–752 C.E. or one year later. He also built gates in the wall, towers, and loopholes (or merlons). Why did Abū Muslim build these walls, and why did he remain in Samarqand for at least one-and-a-half years and probably more than two years?

The first reason was that it was necessary to crush the last remaining velleities/vestiges of independence of the local kings. This was precisely the moment when, as we know from the historical sources, eleven of the kings of Transoxiana attempted for one last time to liberate themselves from Arab power by presenting a request to the Chinese emperor to attack the "Black Clothes," that is, the ʿAbbasids. Many kings were executed, such as Qutayba b. Tughshāda, the king of Bukhara, and Ikhrīd, the king of Kish. The sources are unanimous on one point — it was certainly not only punishment of the rebellious "old-fashioned" kings but a large purge of the noble class of the country. The second cause was the expansion of the Chinese T'ang empire, which culminated in the defeat of the Chinese army by ʿAbbasid general Ziyād b. Sāliḥ in the battle of the Ṭalas River in July 751. Abū Muslim was occupied with the preparations for this campaign in Samarqand. The third cause was a consequence of the foregoing victory. After the Ṭalas River Battle "Abū Muslim planned to undertake incursions into China and he made preparations in view of this." [12] The style and the methods employed by Abū Muslim must have led to a significant change in the city and it is possible that he even considered Samarqand as a base-point on the road to conquering China.

ARCHITECTURAL CONTEXT OF THE BUILDING

At Samarqand there is no doubt that this palace, built in the tradition of Middle Eastern or Iranian architecture, was designed by an architect from the region. The plan has nothing in common with royal buildings of local tradition. We have a relatively good knowledge of Sogdian architecture of the pre-Islamic period thanks to the excavation of three palaces, among others: at Bukhara (Varakhsha), Pendjikent, and Shahristān (Bundjikat), the capital of Ushrusana.

The palaces of Pendjikent and Shahristān are similar (fig. 3.6); the organization of their inner space belongs to a single artistic school. They are composed of a compact series of ceremonial rooms, which are not symmetrically disposed. The main, largest room is a rectangular throneroom (22.80 × 12.25 m at Pendijkent and 17.65 × 11.77 m at Shahristān), situated in the western part of these buildings. In this room a large and deep niche/loggia (4.50 × 4.75 m at Pendjikent) was built in the southern wall and was clearly meant to contain the throne. To the east of the throneroom there was a square ceremonial room (of about 10 × 10 m) with four columns. Both palaces are characterized by the magnificence of their decoration. It is interesting to note that even the orientation of the main rooms is the same at Bundjikat and at Pendjikent. In addition, in both cases access to the throneroom is from the northern side via a long corridor oriented east–west. (The corridors play an important role in the plan of the buildings.)

---

12. Muṭahhar b. Ṭāhir al-Maqdīsī, *Le livre de la création et de l'histoire de Motahhar ben Tāhir el-Maqdīsī*, attributed to Abū Zayd Ahmed ibn Sahl Al-Balkhī, volume 6, edited and translated by Clément Huart (Paris, 1919), pp. 74–75.

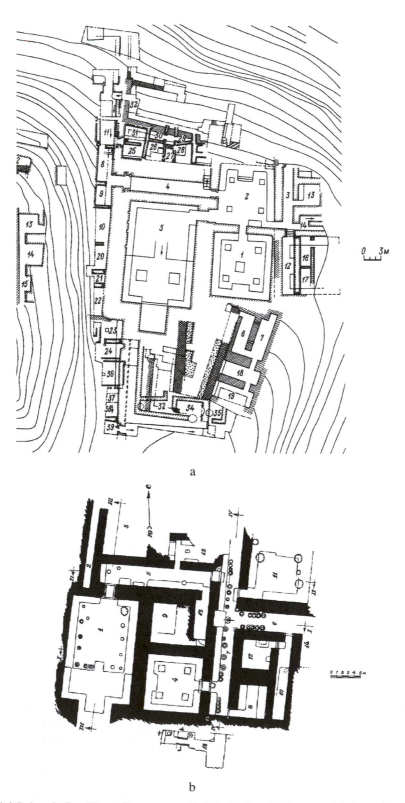

a

b

Figure 3.6. (*a*) Palace in Pendjikent (Raspopova, *Zhilishcha Pendzhikenta*, p. 168) and (*b*) palace in Shahristān (Bundjikat) (Negmatov Negmatov, "Issledovanija v Severnom Tadzhikistane v 1970 g.," *Arxeologischeskie raboty v Tadzhikistane* 10 [1970], Moscow 1973, fig. 11)

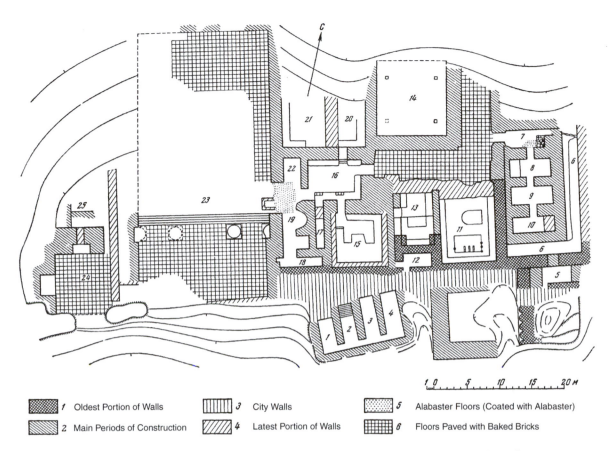

Figure 3.7. Palace in Varakhsha (V. A. Shishkin, *Varakhsha*, Moscow, 1963, fig. 16)

1 Oldest Portion of Walls	*3* City Walls	*5* Alabaster Floors (Coated with Alabaster)
2 Main Periods of Construction	*4* Latest Portion of Walls	*6* Floors Paved with Baked Bricks

These two palaces may be considered as part of the same architectural tradition as the Sogdian house; they mark the "limit" of the development of this type of architecture but are not fundamentally different in any way.[13] This is certainly linked to the level of social, economic, and political relations of the society, and in particular to the relatively high status of the free Sogdian citizen and to the limited nature of the king's supreme power. This type of palatial complex was widely distributed throughout Māwarāʾannahr, for example, in Shāsh (Ak-tepe Junusabadskij).

The palace of the *Bukhārkhudāt* at Varakhsha follows slightly different architectural principles (fig. 3.7); the proximity of Iranian architectural traditions can be seen, for example, in an *iwān* with imposing columns (2 m in diameter), which clearly served as a throneroom. However, even if the palace of Varakhsha is slightly more regular, it does not have anything to do with that of a planned symmetrical complex organized around a central courtyard. It is plausible, however, as Aleksandr Naymark suggests,[14] that the rebuilding of this palace after the Arab conquest can explain such non-Transoxianian elements in the plan (massive columns) and stucco decoration.

It is clear that the kings of the principalities of Transoxiana did not attempt to imitate the imperial style linked to the organization of the royal court (both administrative and ceremonial), which is characteristic of the palatial architecture of Sassanid Iran, for example. There, the

13. Valentina I. Raspopova, *Zhilishcha Pendzhikenta: Opyt istoriko-social'noj interpretatsii* (Leningrad, 1990), p. 182.

14. Aleksandr Naymark, "Returning to Varakhsha," *The Silk Road Foundation Newsletter* 1/2 (2003): 9–22.

domed throneroom was placed in a central (axial) position, whereas its access was marked by the presence (in most cases) of an *iwān*, facing the inner courtyard; for example, the palaces of Imārat-i Khosrow (at Qaṣr-i Shīrīn) and that of Fīrūzabād. This same tradition survived the Arab conquest and is also characteristic of the palaces of the Umayyad and especially ʿAbbasid periods.

SOME REMARKS ON THE ORIGIN OF THE PLAN

A clear correspondence exists between the plan of the governor's residence at Samarqand and the Umayyad castles of Bilād aš-Šām, situated in the now desert regions of Syria and Jordan (Qaṣr al-Ḥayr al-Gharbī and al-Sharqī, Ǧabal Says, Umm al-Walīd, and many others), as well as with the Umayyad palace of Jerusalem and the *bayt*s (*buyūt*) of the *dār al-imāra* at ʿAmmān. A contemporary parallel to the *dār al-imāra* at Samarqand is furnished by the *bayt*s of the palaces of Raqqa (Palace C), where a similar row of massive portico pillars leads out onto a closed courtyard (east and west palaces).

We can consider (given the contemporary state of archaeological research) that the *dār al-imāra* at Samarqand is one of the first administrative buildings in Transoxiana in the Early Middle Ages built around a central courtyard surrounded by a series of symmetrically disposed rooms. Even if it did not exert a direct influence on later buildings, it marks the beginning of a new architectural tradition, of which the lower palace of Khulbuk in Khuttal, dated to the ninth century, and the caravanserai of Paykend, at the end of the eighth/beginning of the ninth century, are good examples, as are the later caravanserais and *madrasas*.

The palace in Samarqand is at the moment one of the oldest known examples of civil "Islamic" architecture in an area stretching between Iran (Mesopotamia) and Māwarāʾannahr. The dating of this monument is based on precise stratigraphic data. Its importance for the study of the Early Islamic period in Khurāsān, a key region of the ʿAbbasid state system, is fundamental since administrative buildings of this period have not yet been found in large oriental towns such as Bukhara, Marw, Balkh, or Nīshāpūr. Indeed, we do not have many examples from the Near East (ʿAmmān, Jerusalem, and Raqqa).

Apart from two administrative buildings in the northern part of the Afrasiab giving evidence of important innovations due to the arrival of the new colonists, the city itself was exposed to the characteristic transformations. As shown by the excavations of Galina Shishkina in the western part of Afrasiab since the mid-eighth century, the urban fabric was beginning to change.[15] The courtyards in a dense residential quarter became a significant element, something which was not, or very rarely, present in the urban fabric of pre-Islamic times (fig. 3.8).

The mid-eighth century is the turning point for the city: architecture aside, we can mention the reoccupation of the quarters abandoned after the Arab conquest, new forms of ceramics (this requires a special study), large-scale production of baked bricks, and particularly the first mint in Samarqand on behalf of the ʿAbbasids; from A.H. 143/760–761 C.E. *fals* were minted in Samarqand by governor Dāʾūd b. Kurāz (Gurāz). The following issue of al-Ashʿath b. Yaḥyā in A.H. 144/761–762 C.E. preserved, with the traditional ʿAbbasid formula and the name of al-Mahdā, a *tamga*, the symbol of the *ikhshīd*s of Samarqand as a last sign of respect towards the ancient dynasty losing political control over the country.

---

15. Galina V. Shishkina, "Gorodskoj kvartal VIII–XI vv. na severo-zapade Afrasiaba," in *Afrasiab* 2, ed- ited by Iakh'ia G. Guliamov, pp. 117–56 (Tashkent, 1973).

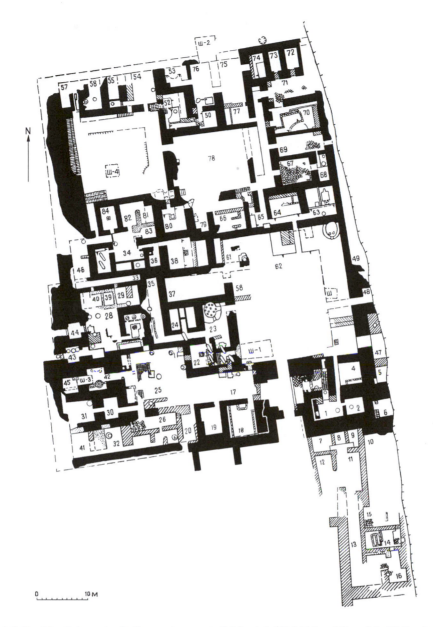

Figure 3.8. Residential quarter in the western part of Afrasiab (Shishkina, "Gorodskoj," fig. 1, p. 119)

CONCLUSION

Māwarāʾannahr never had the traditions of an empire state as such, a fact due to its geopolitical situation between two imperial neighbors, China and Iran. Neither China nor Iran ever held this region for a long period of time. It goes without saying that their influence was notably present there, but nothing was imposed by force. From the eighth century on, the situation was completely changed. In Central Asia, the Arabs succeeded where other empires, such as that of the Sassanids, had failed. They brought the elements of Iranian and Near Eastern tradition into the region directly. In a certain manner, the Arabs carried to Māwarāʾannahr the old-fashioned imperial traditions absorbed during the first century of Hegira by the new Muslim community. The impact of the invasion was sufficiently deep to determine the post-conquest political and cultural evolution of the Central Asian region.

Sughd was thus involved, by force, in a process of integration into the largest empire at that time. This does not mean that everything was imported or that all local things were neglected; on the contrary, Sughd and other regions of Māwarā'annahr played a role as the breeding-ground for the formation of the new culture traditionally called "Muslim." The palaces of Samarqand mark the beginning of this process.[16]

---

16. I would like to express my gratitude to M. S. Stride
      and M. J. Dallett for their kind help in correcting the
      English text of this article.

4

ISLAM, ARCHAEOLOGY, AND SWAHILI IDENTITY

MARK C. HORTON

Department of Archaeology and Anthropology, University of Bristol

The coast of eastern Africa is the home to a remarkable Islamic society, which is known by the general term Swahili.[1] This society, which extends along some 3,000 km between southern Somalia and Mozambique, as well as the offshore islands of Pemba, Zanzibar, Mafia, the Comores, and parts of northern Madagascar, has many definable features in common. These include a common adherence to Sunni Islam and a single language, kiSwahili, as well a common kinship structure based on patrilineal descent groups, and at least in the past, a key role as intermediaries in the international trade of the western Indian Ocean. Another important feature of the Swahili is their urban culture, with stone houses, mosques, and tombs, complex systems of governance, and what is now recognized as a rural hinterland that supplied the towns with trade goods and food supplies.

While traditional Swahili society survives today in pockets along this immense coastline, the archaeological evidence shows that it was once much more extensive. There are approximately 400 sites that contain some form of masonry construction, mostly in the form of mosques and tombs, and about fifty sites that contained stone houses. But this is only part of the story, as recent archaeological survey has shown. For example, in an area of northern Pemba Island, where there were two "stone towns," a 2% sample produced over forty sites — mostly villages with a small number of mud and thatch houses.[2] It appears that ancient populations levels were perhaps even higher than the present-day numbers, which on Pemba is around 150,000.

It is inevitable that our understanding of the Swahili has been richly colored by the ethnographic record gleaned from the places Swahili culture has survived. This has been in the Lamu archipelago, and to some extent on Zanzibar, Pemba, and Mafia. Lamu and the nearby town of Pate are classic "towns" with many stone houses, narrow streets, numerous mosques, and a developed urban Islamic culture.[3] Accounts of the past, largely gleaned from the patrician inhabitants, recall a golden age of prosperity, largely supported through domestic and plantation slavery, in which the privileged classes lived a life of opulence based on a rich imported material culture. This urban culture developed complex cultural expression through Islamic practices of piety and charity, and in the purity of the women and houses, and the honour and reputation of the men.[4] But in many ways this is a constructed past that never quite existed, or if it did, only for a short period in the late eighteenth to mid-nineteenth century.

1. Mark C. Horton and John Middleton, *The Swahili: The Social Landscape of a Mercantile Society* (Oxford, 2000); A. H. J. Prins, *The Swahili-Speaking Peoples of Zanzibar and the East African Coast: Arabs, Shirazi, and Swahili* (London, revised edition, 1967).

2. Jeffrey Fleisher, "Viewing Stonetowns from the Countryside: An Archaeological Approach to Swahili Regional Systems, AD 800–1500" (Ph.D. diss., University of Virginia, 2003), pp. 107–49.

3. John Middleton, *The World of the Swahili: An African Mercantile Civilization* (New Haven, 1992) provides a detailed account of the Swahili viewed from within a largely patrician perspective.

4. Horton and Middleton, *Swahili*, pp. 204–05.

In reality Swahili culture and identity is much more diverse and complex. The "Lamu" based version of Swahili culture is probably very much the exception rather than the rule. For example, widespread slavery seems to have developed in the late eighteenth century in response to Omani settlement on the coast, and the expansion of European slaving interests (mostly French and Portuguese) into the Indian Ocean. Before this time, there is very little evidence that the Swahili kept slaves, beyond the occasional domestic.

Nineteenth century slavery also altered the nature of the traditional rural economy, where, before the plantations the "towns" were placed at the center of a large rural conurbation of settlement.[5] These towns, often located on small islands, produced their own food, often requiring the inhabitants to travel to the mainland or main island to farm. But they also were dependant on a network of Swahili villages that were entirely rural in character, with no stone architecture or sense of town planning. They can be called "Swahili" in that they were inhabited by Muslims, with kinship ties to the main towns. They produced their own food (shellfish and fish, cereals, mostly millets, sorghum and rice, as well as cattle, sheep, and goats) and traded surpluses to the towns in exchange for imported goods and craft items. In some cases the hinterland to the town could be a considerable distance away, as in the case of northern Pemba, which supplied food (mostly rice) to Mombasa. Political control of these Swahili villages by the towns varied considerably; many had economic and religious links to the main towns but had very weak political ties. In other cases the towns set out to control their hinterland, often with mixed success.

However, the conurbations also contained other groups that were linked culturally and economically to the towns, but who were not necessarily Muslim, or even kiSwahili-speaking. This is best seen on the southern Kenyan coast, where the diwans of Vumba controlled a large territory from the mid-eighteenth century, which included a series of Swahili villages (known as "Shirazi" towns, which once had their own rulers but were now dispossessed by the Vumba), as well as non-Muslim farmers such as the Digo and the Segeju.[6] These non-Muslims had a *watani* or joking relationship with the Vumba and supplied agricultural goods as well as military protection to the polity. While militarily weak, the Vumba were able to control these different groups through their access to trade goods and their ritual status as sharifs and were considered to possess Islamic authority, which could be interpreted as magical powers, for example, over rain or healing.

THE CONTRIBUTION OF ARCHAEOLOGY

Documents and traditions often give a static account of a Swahili society, with unchanging social and religious institutions — a society pickled in aspic, viewed through a nineteenth century golden age. In reality most historians and anthropologists concern themselves with the last 200 years and have little interest in the previous 2,000 years.

Archaeologists have been prominent in reconstructing the origins and early history of Swahili society because of the quality of surviving material evidence and the lack of other materials with which to work. The historical sources are partial, with only short descriptions from

---

5. Horton and Middleton, *Swahili*, pp. 136–37; 165–72; Fleisher, "Viewing Stonetowns." In *Swahili*, Horton and Middleton called these rural settlements commoner towns, but in reality they are really villages and in retrospect this is probably a better term.

6. Horton and Middleton, *Swahili*, pp. 166–68; W. F. McKay, "A Precolonial History of the Southern Kenya Coast" (Ph.D. diss., Boston University, 1975); Prins, *Swahili-Speaking Peoples*, p. 94.

outsiders who had scant understanding of how Swahili society functioned.[7] The Swahili's own chronicles and histories, with the exception of one paraphrase recorded by the Portuguese, all date to the later nineteenth century, and although clearly an oral record of earlier generations, are often little more than a listing of the rulers and their activities. Oral traditions can be helpful but are even more recent and can be subject to much interpretation, sometimes wildly speculative.[8] Historical linguistics suggests cultural developments though the study of vocabulary, but there is always a lack of chronological precision in these analyses.[9]

However, the record of archaeologists in reconstructing early Swahili society has itself been controversial. Archaeological research has been undertaken on the eastern African coast since 1948. James Kirkman pioneered a series of excavations at Gedi and the surrounding areas, setting up a National Park there for the colonial government. Kirkman was also invited to undertake a short excavation on Pemba Island, looking for Qanbalu, the town visited by al-Masudi in 916; he later excavated at Kilwa at the request of Gervase Mathew and Sir Mortimer Wheeler, who were keen to locate Roman trade outposts in Africa (as Wheeler had discovered in India).[10] In 1957 Neville Chittick, who had previously worked in Sudan but actually trained as a lawyer, was appointed as the first conservator of antiquities in Tanganyika. In 1960 a British Institute was established (under Wheeler's support) and Chittick became its second director in 1961, where he remained until 1982, undertaking massive excavations at Kilwa as well as in the Lamu archipelago.[11] The Kilwa project was an exercise in historical archaeology, where the various versions of the Kilwa Chronicle were tested against the archaeological and numismatic evidence.[12] Under Chittick and Kirkman, the archaeology of the coast developed a very oriental interpretation. The focus was on stone towns and their architecture, which were assumed to have been founded by overseas merchants (mostly Arabs and Persians), who brought a degree of civilization to the African coast. Gedi was rechristened the "Arab city of Gedi"; Shirazi settlers, who ultimately came from the northern coast of the Persian Gulf, founded Kilwa and Manda.[13] This approach had little time for rural settlement, mud architecture, or indeed "African" pottery, when faced with quantities of Islamic and Chinese imports and well-preserved stone buildings.[14] Curiously neither Chittick nor Kirkman were particularly interested in mosques either. Despite working at Gedi for close to twenty years, Kirkman failed to notice the ruins of the largest

---

7. Most of the sources are conveniently collected and translated in G. S. P. Freeman-Grenville, *The East African Coast: Select Documents from the First to the Earlier Nineteenth Century* (Oxford, 1962).

8. For example, James de Vere Allen, *Swahili Origins: Swahili Culture and the Shungwaya Phenomenon* (London, 1993).

9. Derek Nurse and Thomas Spear, *The Swahili: Reconstructing the History and Language of an African Society, 800–1500* (Philadelphia, 1985); Derek Nurse and Thomas J. Hinnebusch, *Swahili and Sabaki: A Linguistic History* (University of California Publications in Linguistics 121; Berkeley, 1993).

10. James S. Kirkman, *The Arab City of Gedi: Excavations at the Great Mosque, Architecture and Finds* (London, 1954); idem, "Excavations at Ras Mkumbuu on the Island of Pemba," *Tanganyika Notes and Records* 53 (1959), pp. 161–78; idem, "Kilwa – the Cutting Behind the Defensive Wall," *Tanganyika Notes and Records* 50 (1958), pp. 94–101.

11. H. Neville Chittick, *Kilwa: An Islamic Trading City on the East African Coast*, 2 volumes (Memoir of the British Institute in Eastern Africa 5; Nairobi, 1974); H. Neville Chittick, *Manda: Excavations at an Island Port on the Kenya Coast* (Memoir of the British Institute in Eastern Africa 9; Nairobi, 1984).

12. H. Neville Chittick, "The 'Shirazi' Colonization of East Africa," *Journal of African History* 6/3 (1965); Chittick, *Kilwa*, pp. 235–45.

13. Chittick, *Manda*, pp. 219–20.

14. Mark C. Horton, "The Asiatic Colonisation of the East African Coast, the Manda Evidence," *Journal of the Royal Asiatic Society* 1986/2 (1986): 201–13.

mosque on the site.[15] Chittick's work at Manda, which he claimed as the first landfall of the Shirazi settlers, did not include any investigations of the ruined mosque, which while fifteenth century, has earlier building underneath it.

By 1980, some fifteen years after the nations of East Africa had gained their independence from the colonial powers, the "colonial" interpretation of the Swahili was looking somewhat shaky.[16] Historical linguists had been at work on the structure of kiSwahili and showed that it was not a Creole language based on a mixture of Arabic and Bantu, but a full member of the North East Coastal Bantu group languages, with surprisingly few Arab (and virtually no Persian) loanwords.[17] Historians were looking at the oral traditions and saw that they could not be taken literally; indeed several were the product of nineteenth century "arabization" of the coast.[18] The view that civilization could only come from the orient was no longer tenable as a valid archaeological (or indeed historical) interpretation.[19] In many ways, the Swahili coast represented a parallel case to Great Zimbabwe, where similar interpretations hid the clear African context of the site.

SHANGA

It was within these debates that the excavations began at Shanga in 1980 and continued until 1988.[20] Shanga was a typical Swahili stone town located in the Lamu archipelago (fig. 4.1). Chittick surveyed it in 1964, but undertook no further work, concentrating his activities at nearby Manda, which he believed to have been founded by Persians from Siraf. Unlike Manda, Shanga had its complete fourteenth century urban layout preserved, with some 200 houses, three mosques, and around 500 stone tombs. The final population was around 3,000. Many of these houses had plans that were similar to "ethnographically" observed Swahili houses of the eighteenth and nineteenth centuries, including decorated wall niches. The nearby Swahili town of Siyu had among its inhabitants a group that claimed to have been the survivors of Shanga who had settled there when it was overrun by Pate. There was no doubt that Shanga was a fully Swahili stone town.

The detailed layout of the town allowed us to target excavations to see how old Shanga really was and how its plan developed over time. A series of excavations identified upwards of twenty phases of occupation, with a total depth of 4 m of stratigraphy. The bottom levels, dating to about 750 C.E., contained only posthole structures, several of which were circular huts. Of particular interest was the local pottery, representing about 97% of the total, which had close similarities to Iron Age pottery from the interior. One site showed particularly close similarities,

15. Stéphane Pradines, "Islamization and Urbanization on the Coast of East Africa: Recent Excavations at Gedi, Kenya," *Azania* 38 (2003): 180–82.

16. H. Neville Chittick, "The East Coast, Madagascar, and the Indian Ocean," in *The Cambridge History of Africa*, Volume 3, edited by Roland Anthony Oliver (Cambridge, 1977), pp. 183–231, especially p. 218 is probably the last expression of this colonial view of the Swahili.

17. Nurse and Hinnebusch, *Swahili and Sabaki.*

18. Randall L. Pouwels, *Horn and Crescent: Cultural Change and Traditional Islam on the East African Coast 800–1900* (Cambridge, 1987).

19. Thomas Spear, "Early Swahili History Reconsidered," *International Journal of African Historical Studies* 33/2 (2000): 257–89, covers many of the developments during this period.

20. Mark C. Horton, *Shanga: The Archaeology of a Muslim Trading Community on the Coast of East Africa* (London, 1996); idem, "The Early Settlement of the Northern Swahili Coast" (Ph.D. diss., University of Cambridge, 1985).

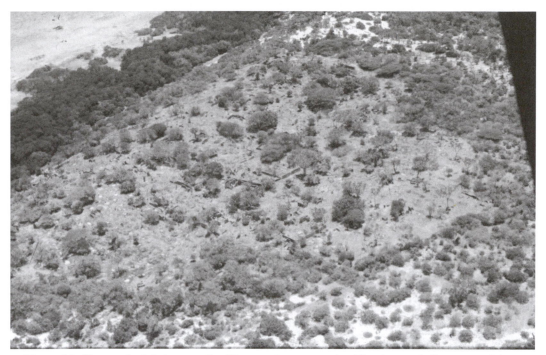

Figure 4.1. Shanga. Aerial photograph of fourteenth century ruins. The site was built over sand dunes (visible in the foreground). The friday mosque is located in the center of the site and the harbor is at the top of the figure

Wenje, on the Tana River, so we defined its ceramics as "Tana tradition," a term that now has widespread acceptance.[21]

The Shanga sequence showed that the Swahili could be traced back to the eighth century and that there was a continuous evolution of ceramics, architecture, and indeed culture. Combined with what is known from other sites, this provides a 1,200 year sequence of Swahili cultural history to the ethnographically observed present.

One criticism of the Shanga project is that it was focused too much on a single site, and the opportunity was not taken to undertake survey of the Lamu archipelago and adjacent mainland. While numerous mud and thatch houses were excavated, the focus of the research remained on a stone town and its immediate environment. Recent research has moved away from this approach to locate and excavate sites that largely contain mud and thatch houses and to recover the hinterland of major sites, showing that they form part of a complex settlement pattern. Locating these sites and their ceramic signatures has provided a different way of looking at Swahili origins.[22]

21. The connection between the coast and the interior for these ceramics was first recognized in D. W. Phillipson, "Some Iron Age Sites in the Lower Tana Valley," *Azania* 14 (1979): 155–60. The pottery is also referred to as "triangular incised ware" because of the dominant motif; Felix Chami, *The Tanzanian Coast in the First Millennium AD: An Archaeology of the Iron-working, Farming Communities* (Studies in African Archaeology 7; Uppsala, 1994). Some writers refer to it as triangular incised ware/Tana tradition (TIW/TT).

22. Jeffrey Fleisher and Adria LaViolette, "Elusive Wattle-and-Daub: Finding the Hidden Majority in the Archaeology of the Swahili," *Azania* 34 (1999): 87–108; Fleisher, "Viewing Stonetowns."

EARLY COASTAL SITES

These early Iron Age communities seem to have been maritime from an early date. Not only do we have the evidence of the *Periplus of the Erythraean Sea* (ca. 40 C.E.) of the local inhabitants using sewn boats, especially around the island of Menouthias, but now also a number of finds of Early Iron Age Kwale pottery from Mafia (associated with a third century carbon-14 date), as well as Kwale and Koma Islands, showing that early Bantu-speaking farmers were also fully able to cross the Mafia channel from the continent.[23] Curiously, there is no transition to Tana tradition on Mafia Island, suggesting that these communities died out by the sixth century.

There has been some uncertainly about the typological status of Tana tradition pottery. Initially it was thought to belong to its own localized ceramic tradition, based along the northern coast, from where Swahili culture was meant to have spread out along the whole eastern coast (according to both the traditions, and the historical linguistics). However, surveys showed that by the eighth century it already had a very widespread distribution, as far south as Mozambique, and as far north as near Mogadishu, as well as to the offshore islands of Zanzibar and Pemba.[24] It was also found inland as far as the Rufigi River and up to 300 miles inland. Often associated with ironworking and located in areas suitable for farming, it seemed likely that this was the main type of early Iron Age pottery of coastal eastern Africa. Detailed statistical analysis of the forms and decoration now show that Tana tradition develops from the early phases of Iron Age pottery dating to the beginning of the first millennium.[25] The typological shift from Kwale to Tana dates to about 500 C.E. and surprisingly few Kwale sherds have been found in Tana sites.

It seems that the Tana sites represent a very different kind of Iron Age society to that of the earlier Iron Age. The coastal sites are clearly exploiting the maritime resources on a massive scale, with extensive fish and shellfish remains. They seem to be involved intensively in shell bead production and ironworking, with some copperworking. The sites can be large, especially on the islands of Zanzibar and Pemba, where deposits can cover up to 30 ha (the earlier Kwale sites cover only a few hectares). Imports, mostly pottery, but also glass, and a few glass and stone beads are found, indicating that these places are participating in long-distance trade. The sites with Tana pottery in the interior seem to have a similar range of craft activity, although relying more heavily on hunted and agricultural resources, while imports are far scarcer.

By the eighth century the eastern African coast was inhabited by quite large populations, especially in particular areas such as around the islands of Zanzibar and Pemba and adjacent mainland, in the Lamu archipelago, the Kilwa archipelago and mainland, and on the Comores. These communities were engaged in the trade of the western Indian Ocean but seem to have been equally successful exploiting maritime resources and maintaining connections with the hinterland.[26]

23. Lionel Casson, *The Periplus Maris Erythraei: Text with Introduction, Translation, and Commentary* (Princeton, 1989); F. A. Chami, "The Early Iron Age on Mafia Island and Its Relationship with the Mainland," *Azania* 34 (1999): 1–10.

24. Horton and Middleton, *Swahili*, p. 42; Chami, *The Tanzanian Coast*.

25. Richard Helm, "Conflicting Histories: The Archaeology of Iron-Working, Farming Communities in the Central and Southern Coast Region of Kenya" (Ph.D. diss., University of Bristol, 2000).

26. Horton and Middleton, *Swahili*, pp. 42–46; on the Kilwa hinterland, S. Wynne-Jones, personal communication. The newly discovered site of Tumbe on northern Pemba covers at least 30 ha; Fleisher and LaViolette, "Elusive Wattle-and-Daub," p. 103.

Figure 4.2. Shanga. Friday mosque, showing the main wall of the prayer hall, with well and washing area
in the foreground. The roof was supported on pillars and made of thatch and timber,
echoing earlier styles of timber mosques

ISLAMIC ARCHAEOLOGY IN EAST AFRICA

Modern archaeological research has tended to examine the African context and origins of
the Swahili and has focused upon these non-Islamic Tana tradition sites. The role of Islam in
Swahili origins has often been confused with ethnicity; Islam = foreignness, or even Islam = Arabs, and attempts to identify early African Islam on the coast has diminished local cultural
achievements. Islam to many coastal archaeologists and historians was of little importance in the
formation of Swahili society — all the elements were already there in those Tana tradition settlements of the coast.[27]

What, however, remains without dispute is that the acceptance of Islam by the coastal societies represents the point at which they become different from the Iron Age communities of the
coastal hinterland and interior. Without exception every pre-nineteenth century mosque or tomb
lies within 1,000 m of the seashore, and Islam drew a very clear divide between the coast and
interior, which before the ninth century enjoyed a degree of cultural unity.

Shanga provides the best archaeological evidence for the origins of Swahili Islam (fig. 4.2).
The survey of the town showed that the settlement was arranged around a rectangular enclosure,
with a well at its center. This well dated to the very beginning of the site and continued in use
throughout its existence. The main mosque was attached to this well and so was also located in
the middle of the town. The study of the fabric of the mosque showed that it was a very complex
multiperiod building dating from about 1000 C.E. The floor rested on a platform of white sand

27. For example, the otherwise excellent Spear, "Early
    Swahili History," barely mentions the impact of Is-
    lamization on coastal communities. See also
    Chapurukha M. Kusimba, *The Rise and Fall of
    Swahili States* (Walnut Creek, 1999) for an account
    of the Swahili that omits virtually all reference to
    Islam.

Figure 4.3. Excavations inside the prayer hall of the Friday mosque at Shanga. The plaster floor dates to around 1000 C.E., while the earlier stone mosque dates to 900 C.E. The sand platform fill contains numerous small silver coins, probably carried with the sand from the town's trading beach

carried from the beach (fig. 4.3), containing datable imports as well as locally minted but minuscule silver coins, giving two names, Muhammad and Abd Allah, and Arabic mottos.[28]

Below the platform were the remains of an earlier stone mosque, in this case with a square prayer hall and a southern room and a western addition. This mosque has a *miḥrāb* but had a

---

28. Horton, *Shanga*, pp. 84–86; the earliest well layer was found in phase one (ibid., p. 117). For the study of the mosques, see ibid., chapters 9–10, and coins, ibid., chapter 18.

different *qibla* line to the later mosque; it dated to about 900 C.E. This was not the earliest mosque on the site but below it were a sequence of seven earlier timber mosques, several with two phases, and again taking a different *qibla* line (fig. 4.4). The floors were made of a local mud carried from the mangrove swamps, and the walls were also of mud, supported on either posts or sticks set in closely set lines. In some cases the roof was supported on a central

Figure 4.4. View of the excavations of the timber mosques at Shanga, showing remains of a ninth century mosque made from small sticks. Note the central posthole. The other postholes belong to later timber phases

posthole. Narrow southern rooms were a particular feature of several of the mosques. One of the mosques comprised only a spread of small pebbles, and no apparent structure. A sequence of carbon-14 dates gives a sequence from the later eighth century to the late ninth century, suggesting that each phase lasted about fifteen years. The conclusion is that Shanga was Islamic from its beginning or very shortly afterwards.

Needless to say this evidence has been controversially received. Allen refuses to accept anything earlier than 900 as possible for the existence of Islam on the coast, as this does not fit into his perceived notions of Swahili history.[29] Peter Garlake seems unhappy with my interpretation, as the area excavated was too small (although the full plans of the buildings were recovered), the buildings do not face Mecca, and they lack *miḥrābs*.[30] But projecting *miḥrābs* only become common in the mid-ninth century (e.g., the first timber mosque at Shanga that has a possible *miḥrāb*, has a large post on the *qibla* wall dating to the late ninth century). The orientation can be carefully explained through a changing geographical knowledge of the relative locations of East Africa and Arabia. The pattern of consistent correction over time, plus the discovery of Islamic burials on the earliest *qibla* line demonstrate that this is where they thought the direction of Mecca lay. The clinching evidence comes from the use of the cubit, which is precise, and is 518 mm for the timber mosques, 540 mm for the first stone mosque, and 534 mm for the final mosque — a sequence that reflects usage in the Islamic world as a whole (fig. 4.5).[31]

Others have suggested that the Shanga mosques were built for the use of visiting merchants and not for the local inhabitants, who it is supposed continued to follow traditional religious practices. So to Michael Pearson, the mosque was "for the use of visiting or even resident Arab merchants; the local population was converted later";[32] to David Whitehouse, the mosque was used by "an elite minority of Muslims from Western Asia."[33] However, this is unlikely for a number of reasons. Firstly, the mosque was located in the very center of the site, in what has been reconstructed as central enclosure, largely empty of habitation. It was carefully placed over a large tree stump that had been deliberately burnt, while the natural sand contained flecks of charcoal, indicating that this area had been cleared of vegetation. This area may have been a sacred grove that was cleared to accommodate the new mosque. A mosque for visitors would be located at the edge of the settlement, not in the center, and not at such an important location.

But there is other evidence, which comes from the two earliest burials, dating to the early ninth century. One was of a child, and the second is likely also a child. The silver coins that seem to have been locally minted in the ninth century give the names Muhammad and Abd Allah, which are often associated with recent converts to Islam (fig. 4.6). A small seal stone found in these early levels also proclaims the Islamic nature of the inhabitants.[34]

There does, however, remain a problem, as the small timber mosques had a capacity of between ten and twenty-five worshippers, while estimates of the total population of early Shanga would have been several hundred. So it has been assumed that the mosque served only an elite group of Muslims. Mosque capacities of about 10% of the total population is nonetheless a con-

29. Allen, *Swahili Origins*, p. 36, note 4.

30. Peter S. Garlake, *Early Art and Architecture of Africa* (Oxford, 2002), p. 170.

31. Horton, *Shanga*, pp. 227–28.

32. Michael N. Pearson, *Port Cities and Intruders: The Swahili Coast, India and Portugal in the Early Modern Era* (Baltimore, 1998), p. 15.

33. David Whitehouse, "East Africa and the Maritime Trade of the Indian Ocean, AD 800–1500," in *Islam in East Africa: New Sources: Archives, Manuscripts and Written Historical Sources, Oral History, Archaeology*, edited by Bianca S. Amoretti (Rome, 2001), pp. 411–24, p. 417.

34. Horton, *Shanga*, p. 118; for the seal ring, see ibid., p. 357, fig. 275g.

SHANGA

Development of Mosques

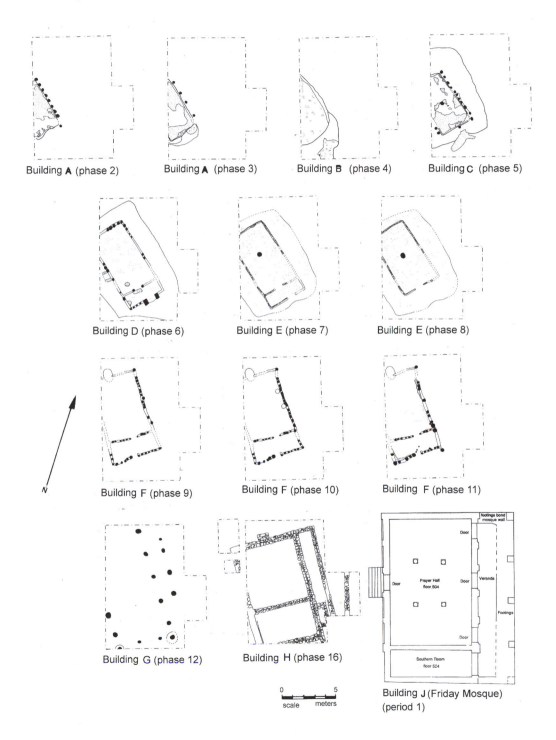

Figure 4.5. Plan of the sequence of mosques excavated at Shanga, dating from 750 to 1000 C.E.

Figure 4.6. Minuscule silver coins from Shanga (diameter 9 mm) dating to the ninth century

sistent figure on the Swahili coast. The final mosque at Shanga held about 300 worshippers (309 sq. m) but the total urban population was about 3,000. In Lamu, the Friday mosque could contain about 500 worshippers, but at its peak the town had a population of around 18,000. In 1985, the stone town contained 4,563 inhabitants, and this must be close to the non-slave population in the nineteenth century.[35] Clearly every adult male does not attend the Friday sermon nowadays, nor did so in the past.

The archaeological evidence suggests that Islam was widely followed by the Shanga population in the late eighth century and was not confined to an elite ruling (or mercantile) group. This was a Muslim settlement made up from African converts — converts who seem to have accepted Islam within a decade or so of the settlement's foundation.

THE ACCEPTANCE OF ISLAM

The process of conversion of the coastal communities remains controversial, as this is something that can also be inferred and partly reconstructed from the historical sources, although often crucial pieces of evidence are missing to make up the complete picture. The archaeological evidence does allow in certain circumstances for us to go beyond the simplistic recognition of Islam, to more specific identification of Shi'ite, Sunni, or Ibadi presence, groups with whom the Swahili had active trading connections from the eighth century. This does provide a way of understanding some of the historical evidence within its Islamic context. This I have done

---

35. Francesco Siravo and Ann Pulver, *Planning Lamu: Conservation of an East Africa Seaport* (Nairobi, n.d.), p. 63.

elsewhere in detail,[36] where my discussion has been much criticized by historians and archaeologists.

Timothy Insoll dislikes any attempt to develop these interpretations or my attempts to make sense of the complex historical record, preferring a rather simplistic "phased" model of conversion, which disregards the Swahili's own oral traditions and chronicles, external sources written in the Islamic world, or indeed a considerable amount of modern historical scholarship on the subject. Recently Justin Willis has echoed these sentiments as "too much willingness to pursue entertaining speculations based upon minimal evidence, notably regarding the alleged presence of Shi'ism along the coast in the early Islamic period."[37] On the other hand, the well-read African Islamic historian Randall Pouwels accepts that the "likelihood that heterodoxy existed in these regions at this time seems high; therefore these accounts have some ring of truth about them."[38]

The main difficulty is that the Swahili have largely followed orthodox Sunni practices since at least the fourteenth century.[39] In the nineteenth century the Omani Arabs introduced Ibadism, and Indian traders introduced Ismaili and Bohra Islam, but this had little impact beyond their own communities. The strength of Sunni practices was established by a complex pattern of migration from around 1200 of sayyids and sharifs from southern Arabia. Mogadishu was one important center, with the Qahtani Wa'il and Fakhr ad-Din clans established from the early thirteenth century. The Mahdali clan, who originated from the Wadi Surdud, were at Kilwa by 1280, when they became sultans but were also in Barawa, Lamu, Pate, and Mombasa. Ibn Battuta, who visited eastern Africa in 1331, noted that Mombasa and Kilwa followed Sunni-Shafi Islam.[40] Another group of sharifs settled in Pate, Lamu, and the Comores in the late sixteenth century, followed by others to Pemba and Zanzibar Islands.

This was not a large-scale migration of Arabs to East Africa, but often single individuals who settled and established substantial lineages. But the impact was the removal of sectarian and non-Islamic practices and the development of the coast as a center of Islamic learning and sanctity. It is not surprising that there is little evidence of early Ibadi and Shi'ite Islam in present day Swahili Islam.[41] It is also likely that many of the Swahili chronicles were composed within these Sunni communities so that accounts of early heterodoxy are garbled and confused. This is a complex early history that archaeological evidence is now beginning to recover.

A good example of how archaeological evidence can reconstruct religious affiliation can be seen with the Ibadis. Mosques constructed by Ibadi settlers from Oman in nineteenth century Zanzibar contain very simple *mihrāb*s, with little decoration, set within the thickness of the *qibla* wall.[42] The theological justification for this is that within the Ibadi rite, no one person should lead the prayers (excepting the elected Imam in Muscat), so the *mihrāb* space should not allow

36. Horton and Middleton, *Swahili*, pp. 47–71; Mark C. Horton, "The Islamic Conversion of the Swahili coast 750–1500," in *Islamic in East Africa: New Sources*, edited by Bianca S. Amoretti (Rome, 2001), pp. 449–69.

37. Justin Willis, "Review of *The Swahili*, by Mark C. Horton and John Middleton," *Azania* 38 (2004): 207–08.

38. Randall L. Pouwels, "The East African Coast, c. 780–1900 CE," in *The History of Islam in Africa*, edited by Nehemia Levtzion and Randall L. Pouwels (Athens, 2000), pp. 251–72, p. 256.

39. Horton and Middleton, *Swahili*, pp. 68–70.

40. Freeman-Grenville, *Select Documents*, pp. 27–32.

41. Thomas Spear, "Review of *The Swahili*, by Mark C. Horton and John Middleton," *International Journal of African Historical Studies* 33/3 (2000).

42. A. Sheriff, "Mosques, Merchants and Landowners in Zanzibar Stone Town," *Azania* 27 (1992): 1–20; Helen Little, "The Nature of the Zanzibar Mosque" (Ph.D. diss., University of Brighton, 1995).

Figure 4.7. Staircase minaret at the eleventh century mosque of Kaole (Tanzania). The absence of tower minarets in East Africa may indicate Ibadi influence in mosque design

this to happen. Similar concerns result in their mosques rarely containing minbars or tower minarets, which are still rare in coastal Swahili architecture (fig. 4.7).

A number of these features can be found in early mosques. The ruined mosque at Sanje ya Kati near to Kilwa, a site dating to the eleventh–twelfth century has the *miḥrāb* set within the thickness of the wall built to double thickness to accommodate it.[43] Two examples are also known from Pemba Island. At Ras Mkumbuu, an excavated early mosque of the tenth century (sealed below an eleventh century mosque) had a very similar plan (fig. 4.8), with a double thickness *qibla* wall, although the area of the *miḥrāb* itself had been robbed out.[44] Excavations in 2004 at the north Pemban site of Chwaka located a twelfth century mosque sealed below a fifteenth century building that also contained a *miḥrāb* niche contained within the thickness of the wall. Perhaps the most interesting example is at Tumbatu, where the Friday mosque has a large conventional *miḥrāb* (fig. 4.9) but with a subsidiary *miḥrāb* at the end of an added (probably in the early thirteenth century) eastern side chamber, which was set within the thickness of the wall. This suggests the presence of a minority community of Ibadis. The historical record provides a possible circumstance for this. At exactly this time the Ibadi community at Kilwa seems to have lost influence, and the sultan of Kilwa, Hasan bin Sulaiman (who may have been an Ibadi), was exiled in the "land of Zanzibar" for fourteen years. The side chamber may have been specially built for the refugee ruler and his followers.

43. Neville Chittick, "Kilwa, a Preliminary Report," *Azania* 1 (1966): 1–37, especially p. 30.

44. Horton and Middleton, *Swahili*, p. 66; Mark C. Horton, *Zanzibar and Pemba: The Archaeology of an Indian Ocean Archipelago* (London, forthcoming).

Figure 4.8. Excavations of the mosque sequence at Ras Mkumbuu (Pemba Island). Below the floor of a large mosque dating to 1050 are the remains of a small stone mosque, the north wall of which had been robbed out, but was of double thickness, suggesting an Ibadi-style *miḥrāb*. Below is an earlier timber building, which may have been the first mosque on the site dating to the early tenth century

The presence of Shi'ites is more difficult to locate. There seems to be few specific features in mosque architecture to go on. There are two styles of *miḥrāb* that seem to be broadly contemporary with one another and may reflect differences in religious doctrine: one that is very elaborate and highly decorated with inscriptions and carved coral (and later Chinese bowls), and a second that is plain with minimal decoration, which may be associated with Sunni-Shafi communities.

Coins possibly provide an alternative indicator with their names and mottos, and these have been minted since the ninth century (fig. 4.10). The Mtambwe series are of interest as several of the names are of Old Testament origin, a possible indicator of Shi'ite associations, while one of the early Kilwa coins has a motto that translates as "Trusts in the Lieutenant of God" — a clear Shi'ite meaning. The small silver coins from early Shanga have technical similarities to both the coins produced by the (Shi'ite) Zaidites of southern Arabia and to those made by (Sunni) Amirs of Sind and the nearby (Ismaili) Fatimids of Multan.[45] In reality, very little is known of these minuscule issues, which have been rarely recovered from excavations and may well have been even more widely produced around the trading communities of the western Indian Ocean.

It is all too easy to dwell on the various comings and goings of different religious groups on the Swahili coast, without appreciating the underlining continuities that were certainly present. There is a strong suspicion that religious doctrine was strongly allied to political action (as seems to have been the case in early thirteenth century Kilwa), which is recorded in the various chronicles and traditions. But the actors were all Swahili Muslims, who played out (and indeed continue) the controversies and conflicts of the Islamic world within their own micro-world of coastal Islam. The real archaeological message is of continuity from the conversions from eighth century onwards. So mosques retain the same basic proportions as the early timber mosques of

45. H. W. Brown, "Coins of East Africa: An Introductory Survey," *Yarmouk Numismatics* 5 (1993): 9–16; "Early Muslim Coinage in East Africa: The Evidence from Shanga," *Numismatic Chronicle* (1992): 83–87; "The Coins," in Horton, *Shanga*, pp. 368– 77; Mark C. Horton, H. W. Brown, and W. A. Oddy, "The Mtambwe Hoard," *Azania* 21 (1986): 115–23; Nicholas M. Lowick, "Fatimid Coins of Multan," *Numismatic Digest* 3 (1983): 62–69.

Figure 4.9. A simple Ibadi *miḥrāb* in a small contemporary mosque at Tumbe (Pemba Island).
The niche is marked in plaster, but no recess is in the wall

Figure 4.10. Part of the Mtambwe hoard (Pemba Island). The associated dinars give a deposition date
after 1066 C.E. Over 2,000 silver coins were found, locally minted in the names of ten local rulers

Figure 4.11. The *miḥrāb* at the thirteenth century mosque of Ras Mkumbuu (Pemba Island) is typical of many examples made from carved coral but with very simple decoration

Shanga. Southern rooms, another early feature, continue in use in contemporary mosques. An echo of the timber and thatch origins of Swahili mosques is reflected in wall pilasters, unnecessary thatched roofs, and internal round timber columns. *Miḥrāb* designs dating to the twelfth century inspire examples in the eighteenth and the nineteenth century as well as contemporary buildings (figs. 4.11–12). Minarets are still absent on mosques, except where money from the Gulf has been used to impose foreign styles — styles that are often poorly received locally.

SWAHILI SPIRITS

As the sharif movement swept away heterodoxy, so also were traces of surviving non-Islamic practices removed. Within the archaeological record there is very little trace of syncretism of African religious practices within coastal Islam. Indeed most of the evidence for such practice comes from modern contexts, where spirits play an important part in Swahili religion (fig. 4.13). There are two main categories of spirit, *mizimu* and *majini*. *Mizimu* are considered more African and linked to landscape and ancestors. They are given small offerings and it is hoped that they will help the owner or farmer, or at least not make her or him ill. *Majini* are more Arabian and linked to Islamic systems of belief, however loosely. *Mapepo* are one type of *majini*, which can have personal names and can possess people and have associations with ruined settlements, especially mosques and tombs. Most Swahili do not consider that their belief in spirits is incompatible with the Islamic faith.

It appears that belief in spirits expanded in the mid-nineteenth century in response to the settlement of slaves from the African interior, and they have become much more widespread since the abolition of slavery in the late nineteenth century. Particular locations are well known

Figure 4.12. The very elaborate *miḥrāb* at Kizimkazi (Zanzibar Island) that has a date of A.H. 500
(1107 C.E.) and which is now considered to be largely of this date. It is very much more
complex than many Swahili *miḥrāb*s, and these may reflect doctrinal differences

for spirit activity and perhaps the most well known is Pemba Island.[46] It is here that early evidence for spirits can be suggested.

46. Linda Giles, "Spirit Possession on the Swahili
     Coast: Peripheral Cults or Primary Texts?" (Ph.D.
     diss., University of Texas at Austin, 1989); Horton
     and Middleton, *Swahili*, pp. 70–71, 190–94. For an
     early description of spirits on Pemba, see William
     H. Ingrams, *Zanzibar: Its History and Its People*
     (London, 1931), pp. 435–40.

Figure 4.13. Baobab tree located at Mbaraki (Mombasa Island, Kenya) that is believed to be a location of spirits, which has been festooned in rag cloths. In the background is the stone tower that was attached to a small mosque, and which may have given the location its reputation

At the fifteenth century enclosed site of Pujini, excavations by Adria LaViolette studied a man-made cave, entered down steps. A carved *siwa* or side-blown horn marked the entrance (fig. 4.14).[47] When it was excavated in the early 1900s, the fill was described as "full of bones of oxen, broken pottery sherds, remnants of wood fires, and two fragments of lamps of coarse earthenware."[48] LaViolette suggests that this was a spirit cave, specially constructed within this palace-like complex. Spirits were often believed to live in underground caves, which are common in the limestone formations of the coast and islands, and this seems to be the most convincing explanation for the Pujini shrine.[49]

In 2004 we were able to excavate an intact deposit that was placed within the *miḥrāb* of a ruined mosque at Chwaka in northern Pemba (fig. 4.15). The deposit was placed on the plaster floor, sealed by loam deposits,[50] and comprised of three elements: a cooking bowl, which had two large pieces of two other vessels covering it, nearby was a hand-grinding stone, and a seashell. In the same deposit was a sherd of Chinese pottery, taken from the bowls that decorated the *miḥrāb* (fig. 4.16). This gives an interesting date as all the bowls had been removed by 1920 and the *miḥrāb* was filled with rubble.[51] The style of the local pottery that makes up the deposit

47. Adria LaViolette, "Swahili Archaeology on Pemba Island, Tanzania, Pujini, Bandari ya Faraji and Chwaka, 1997/1998," *Nyame Akuma* 44: 59–65.

48. Francis B. Pearce, *Zanzibar: The Island Metropolis of Eastern Africa* (London, 1920), p. 381.

49. Ingrams, *Zanzibar*, p. 437.

50. I am very grateful to Drs. Fleisher and LaViolette for inviting me to participate on their project at Chwaka/Tumbe in July 2004, and for allowing me to mention this discovery in advance of their own publications.

51. Pearce, *Zanzibar*, p. 397.

Figure 4.14. *Siwa* (or side-blown horn) decorating the "shrine" at Pujini (Pemba Island) made in plaster relief. This underground chamber may represent a "spirit cave"

Figure 4.15. Deposit within *miḥrāb* of mosque at Chwaka (Pemba Island), comprising a bowl, covering sherds, a seashell, a hand-grinding stone, and a piece of Chinese pottery

Figure 4.16. Detail of the *miḥrāb* deposit from Chwaka

is probably seventeenth or eighteenth century. This pot contained the spirit (hence it had to be covered and contained) and this is part of the tradition of the burial of fingo pots found all along the coast, which contained prophylactic magic to protect special places such as doorways or gateways. The shell is an offering made to a sea spirit, while the grinding stone referred to a domestic spirit. The offering was placed with a *miḥrāb* recess that was similar to a cave; the mosque itself must have gone out of use and was already much ruined.

ISLAMIC ARCHAEOLOGY IN EASTERN AFRICA

Recently, Timothy Insoll has encouraged us to study the archaeology of Islam, both globally and within sub-Saharan Africa, and certainly his compendium of material allows us to look at Islamic practice within the wider study of material culture and society. Yet there remains the considerable difficulty faced by Africanists as to whether we should separate out Islamic societies from their surroundings in either space or time. In the case of the Swahili, this is a very real problem; some, including many Swahili themselves, would claim that their Swahili identity was only formed when they accepted the Islamic faith. Archaeologists and historians prefer to make no such distinction, seeing a seamless transition from pre-Islamic times, and claim that Islam had little impact on a society that already had many features akin to Islam, such as the belief in a single supreme god, and that conversion "demanded little intellectual change — something closer to a reorientation of spiritual solemnization than to a conceptual shift."[52]

One wonders whether the real reason behind this view is that it remains very difficult to recognize Islamic or indeed non-Islamic societies through the archaeological record. Some sites are clearly non- (or pre-) Islamic as they are simply too early in date to be Islamic, while others (e.g., Unguja Ukuu on Zanzibar) spanning the sixth–ninth centuries are likely to have undergone conversion, but this is not really visible in the material culture of the sites. It may be possible to infer changes in pottery types, for example, the shift away from large jars that may have been used for making beer, to smaller bowls and tablewares,[53] but at present the location of mosques and burials remain the only reliable indicator of conversion.

There is also a similar issue when we view these societies spatially. By focusing on the Islamic communities alone, we tend to draw a distinction from those that remain non-Islamic. However, there have been complex relationships within the hinterland that have existed for at least a millennium and probably from the first settlement of the coastal region by farmers 2,000–3,000 years ago. When we ignore these relationships we fall into the sort of narratives that the colonial historians were writing about the civilized coastal communities and the impenetrable "nyika" forest that blocked all communications with the interior. But this was only a barrier to Europeans trying to build railways and roads, and the new archaeological surveys are showing just how much connections did exist along the entire coastline.

The conclusion that we need to make is that Islam was important, but that when we study it in sub-Saharan Africa we have to do so within the framework of a complex understanding of African society as a whole. To archaeologists, this challenge is particularly acute.

---

52. Pouwels, "East African Coast," p. 254; Horton and Middleton, *Swahili*, pp. 176–78.

53. Fleisher, "Viewing Stonetowns," pp. 264–65, 416–18.

5

SYNCRETISM, TIME, AND IDENTITY: ISLAMIC ARCHAEOLOGY IN WEST AFRICA

TIMOTHY INSOLL

School of Art History and Archaeology,
University of Manchester

INTRODUCTION

This paper seeks a brief introduction to the research this author has been completing in the West African state of Mali over the course of the past decade. However, what is presented is not intended to be a fieldwork report, as the primary results have already been published extensively elsewhere.[1] Rather, the focus is upon presenting the relevance of these results within their wider context, both in West Africa, and to a lesser extent, sub-Saharan Africa as a whole.[2]

That the archaeological study of Islam should involve more than a focus upon the explicit indicators of the religion, for example, mosques, inscriptions, and artwork, should now be regarded as commonplace. The influence of religion can be all-encompassing and can potentially influence all aspects of life, including diet, dress, domestic architecture, landscape, and settlement form.[3] This statement obviously does not apply to Islam alone but can be applicable to many other religions as well.[4]

Yet the potential of religion as a primary structuring agent for the archaeological record is often ignored. Two factors can be suggested for the reticence in recognizing religion as a potential superstructure into which all other aspects of life might be placed. Firstly, it can be suggested, a problem lies with the term "religion" itself. Archaeologists appear frightened of using it as a descriptive device, and hence recourse is made to "ritual" where such material is considered, "ritual" being the archaeologists' favorite catchall category for "odd" or otherwise not understood behavior.[5] Hence the implications of "religion" as a term appears little understood, be it in application to Islam or otherwise. But besides the definitional conundrum that it generates — when is archaeological material "religious" as opposed to "ritual" in nature, for example — it can be further suggested that the frequent absence of religion in archaeological interpretation, certainly as an all-inclusive structuring agent, is also perhaps a reflection of many

1. Timothy Insoll, *Islam, Archaeology and History, A Complex Relationship: The Gao Region (Mali) ca. AD 900–1250* (Cambridge Monographs in African Archaeology 39; British Archaeological Reports, International Series 647; Oxford, 1996); idem, *Urbanism, Archaeology and Trade: Further Observations on the Gao Region (Mali): The 1996 Fieldseason Results* (British Archaeological Reports, International Series 829; Oxford, 2000); idem, "The Archaeology of Post Medieval Timbuktu," *Sahara* 13 (2002): 7–22.

2. See also Timothy Insoll, *The Archaeology of Islam in Sub-Saharan Africa* (Cambridge, 2003).

3. Timothy Insoll, *The Archaeology of Islam* (Oxford, 1999).

4. See Timothy Insoll, editor, *Archaeology and World Religion* (London, 2001).

5. Timothy Insoll, *Archaeology, Ritual, Religion* (London, 2004).

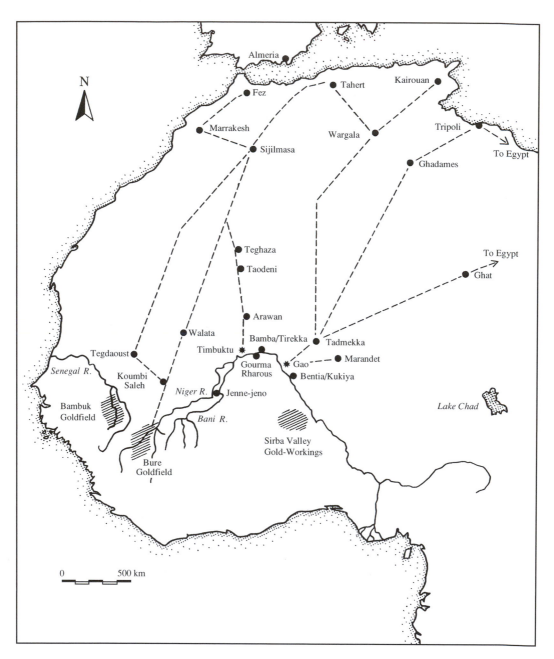

Figure 5.1. The location of Gao (and other centers) in West Africa

archaeologists' worldview themselves; often largely a secular one. Hence in turn this might be projected onto the past, even if inappropriate.

Thus with regard to Islamic archaeology, the resulting interpretation might acknowledge religion, Islam, as significant but reduce its importance to the types of overtly "religious" material culture already described, rather than providing the holistic examination that Islamic belief and practice frequently demand. In support of this one need only draw upon the frequently cited maxim, "Islam is more than a religion but a way of life." Recovery of the latter was precisely the focus of the archaeological research completed in Mali: the potential impact of Islam as a structuring agent for all facets of life, but with the allied aims of also assessing, largely via archaeo-logical evidence, how Islam has helped in the creation of overall social identity in this region, and crucially, fused with African traditional religions in a syncretic process to create African Islam(s).

THE ARCHAEOLOGICAL PROJECT

Archaeological excavations and survey have been focused upon Gao, a major city on the bend of the Niger River in the Sahel region in the east of Mali, and to a lesser extent, the city of Timbuktu, situated some 10 km north of the Niger River on the fringe of the Sahara Desert (fig. 5.1). Both cities were extensively involved in trans-Saharan trade in what would be called in European contexts, the medieval period, but is more correctly referred to in African contexts as the Middle and Late Iron Age. For reasons of descriptive simplicity the term "medieval" will be used here.

SETTLEMENT

Whereas Timbuktu is a name familiar to many, perhaps as a synonym for the remote and mysterious, even if they are unsure whether it is a real place and where exactly it is located, Gao is little known outside of West Africa. However, in terms of historical importance it can be ar-gued that Gao is much more significant than Timbuktu, being the capital of the Songhai empire, the last of the three great medieval West African empires of Ghana (ca. eighth–eleventh centu-ries C.E), Mali (twelfth–fourteenth centuries C.E), and Songhai (fifteenth–sixteenth centuries C.E). Yet the origins of Gao predate its high point under the Songhai empire. It seems in fact to have been founded in the sixth–seventh centuries C.E, thus before Muslim merchants and mis-sionaries began to reach the Western Sahel, a process beginning in the late eighth century when historical sources record contacts between the Ibadi imamate of Tahert (in modern Algeria) and Gao.[6]

Consequently the city was indigenously founded, probably by what are best termed the proto-Songhai,[7] contrary to earlier interpretations that might have seen innovations such as ur-banism as externally derived from North Africa, and transmitted across the Sahara via Muslim traders.[8] This notion of indigenous origins is a factor of importance in reconsidering the whole concept of Islamic identity in the region, in its indigenous nature, or rather how Islam was indig-enously adapted to fit local requirements; it is seemingly a crucial element in the initial acceptance of Islam not only in this region, but in a pattern certainly mirrored through much else of sub-Saharan Africa as well.[9]

At Gao, archaeological evidence for conversion to Islam prior to about the beginning of the tenth century is absent. Thereafter there is an increase in archaeological evidence attesting to contacts with the Muslim world. Items such as glazed pottery, glass vessels, glass beads, and

---

6. T. Lewicki, "Part 1: The Ibádi Community at Basra and the Origins of the Ibádite States in Arabia and North Africa, Seventh–Ninth Centuries. Part 2: The Ibádites in North Africa and the Sudan to the Four-teenth Century," *Cahiers d'Histoire Mondiale* 13 (1971): 51–130.

7. Insoll, *Islam, Archaeology and History.*

8. See, for example, Raymond Mauny, *Tableau géographique de l'Ouest africain au Moyen Age, d'après les Sources écrites, la tradition et l'archéologie* (Mémoires de l'Institut français d'Afrique noire 61; Dakar, 1961).

9. Insoll, *Sub-Saharan Africa.*

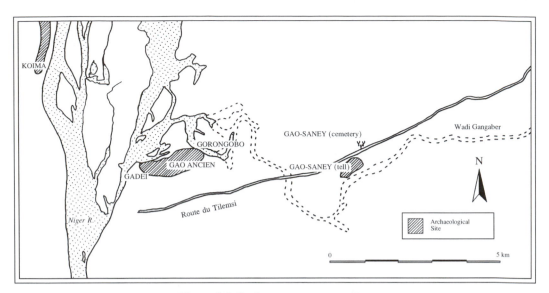

Figure 5.2. Settlement structure at Gao

brass metalwork, goods obtained via Muslim controlled trans-Saharan trade directed through North Africa and Egypt are all found at sites such as Gao.[10] Secondly, the first direct evidence for the presence of Muslims in the Western Sahel is found after this date; evidence already mentioned such as mosques, Muslim burials, and the remains of domestic structures that might have been built according to Muslim social requirements.[11]

Initially, settlement at Gao appears to have been separated; Muslims at the tell site of Gao-Saney, non-Muslims at Gao proper, specifically at the sites of Gadei and Gao Ancien placed some 7 km away from Gao-Saney and situated close to the Niger River (figs. 5.2–3). But the existence of dual settlements persisted after Islam had spread to the inhabitants of Gao Ancien in the late eleventh–twelfth centuries and was possibly due to security concerns — keeping potential nomad raiders at a distance from Gao Ancien, certainly a factor of later consequence.[12]

TRADE

A reason for these safety concerns would have been, conceivably, protecting wealth gained through trans-Saharan trade. Trade was the agency, as noted, by which Islam was initially transferred to the Western Sahel, either by the merchants themselves or by missionaries accompanying, preceding, or following them. A wide range of evidence has been recovered from the excavations at Gao attesting to the operation of this trade, the bulk of which is from Gao Ancien. Besides allowing an insight into potential trade partners with which the merchants of Gao were connected on the other side of the Sahara, this evidence also indicates that the trade seems to have been far removed from a colonial-type system run by groups of North African merchants. Because, as with much of the other evidence recovered, it reinforces the picture of the indigenous nature of the city, its control, and its operation.

10. Insoll, *Islam, Archaeology and History*; idem, "Islamic Glass from Gao, Mali," *Journal of Glass Studies* 40 (1998): 77–88; idem, *Urbanism*.

11. See Insoll, *Archaeology of Islam*.

12. Timothy Insoll, "Iron Age Gao: An Archaeological Contribution," *Journal of African History* 38/1 (1997): 1–30.

Figure 5.3. View of the Niger River from Gao. Photograph by Timothy Insoll

Possibly the most spectacular evidence for the export trade found was a cache of over fifty hippopotamus tusks uncovered in a context dated to the mid-ninth century in Gao Ancien. The hypothesis has been advanced that these tusks represent a consignment of ivory placed on beams within the pit in which they were found, and which was awaiting shipment to the ivory workshops of North Africa but was never sent for reasons that remain unclear.[13] A substantial ivory trade certainly existed between West and North Africa but is little mentioned in the Arabic sources, possibly due to disapproval from more orthodox Muslims, who likewise condemned the use of feathers, horns, hoofs, or tusks derived from animals that were not ritually slaughtered.[14] For example, the North African jurist Ibn Abi Zayd al-Qayrawani (d. 996) specifically mentions that the use of elephant's tusk is expressly disapproved.[15] Nevertheless, large quantities of ivory were certainly used in the workshops of the Maghreb, Islamic Spain, and Egypt, and it is mentioned in Arabic herbals (such as Ibn al-Baytar and Al-Antaki) as having a variety of beneficial qualities.[16]

Evidence for the extensive gold trade that is recorded in the Arabic historical sources is more elusive, which is not surprising considering its ease of recyclability as a material of enduring value. In Gadei a small gold bead was found, while the discovery on the surface at Gao

13. Timothy Insoll, "A Cache of Hippopotamus Ivory at Gao, Mali, and a Hypothesis of its Use," *Antiquity* 69 (1995): 327–36.

14. Nehemiah Levtzion and J. F. P. Hopkins, *Corpus of Early Arabic Sources for West African History*, translated by J. F. P. Hopkins (Fontes Historiae Africanae, Series Arabica 4; Cambridge, 1980), p. 55.

15. John O. Hunwick, "Comment by John Hunwick," *Saharan Studies Association Newsletter* 2 (1994): 11.

16. I am grateful to a reviewer of this paper for pointing this out.

Ancien of a gold *mithqal* coin of North African origin dating from 952–975 has been reported.[17] Equally, evidence for the historically documented slave trade has also proven elusive. Much more abundantly testified are items sourced from North Africa, the Near East, and in certain instances, even further afield. These include glass and glazed pottery, primarily recovered from Gao Ancien and dating from the eleventh to twelfth centuries.[18] Other trade commodities found include hundreds of glass beads, carnelian beads, cowry shells, and brass ingots (fig. 5.4), the latter a material not produced in sub-Saharan Africa and hence a good indicator of long-distance trade.

Overall, the picture of trade, though skewed in favor of more durable commodities for obvious reasons of archaeological survival, is broadly in agreement with that recorded in the Arabic historical sources.[19] If this evidence were to be considered on its own or solely in association with the fired-brick architectural tradition recorded in Gao Ancien, then it might be suggested that Gao was a colonial entrepot run purely to satisfy the requirements of a presumably foreign elite. However, the approach that has been adopted here, that is, treating Gao in its entirety and maximizing what can be gained from all aspects of the archaeological record, indicates that such a premise is flawed, as noted earlier. This was, admittedly, a trade controlled by elites, as might be expected in the capital of what was to become the Songhai empire, but one controlled by a local elite, many of whom had converted to Islam.

INSCRIPTIONS

Initially, Muslim merchants appear to have occupied Gao-Saney, a site complex comprising a tell and associated Muslim cemeteries and tombs, which has not been as intensively investigated as Gao Ancien.[20] The first direct evidence for the presence of Muslims in this region was found here and consists of various inscribed Muslim tombstones that date from ca. 1100–1300. Five of these stelae found at Gao-Saney were imported ready-carved from Muslim Spain in the early twelfth century. These bear both names and dates, and the marble used seems to be from the vicinity of Almeria on the southern Spanish coast.[21]

Yet besides providing further evidence for the operation of trans-Saharan trade between Gao and Almoravid-controlled Spain, these imported stelae also indicate that they were used for purposes other than commemorating the dead because they seem also to have been used to proclaim the new found faith of Islam. We can discern this as three of the kings commemorated on the stelae in the cemetery at Gao-Saney, including two of the imported Spanish examples, were recent converts to Islam. Their new identity, and indeed their piety, were clearly shown by

17. J. Latruffe, "Au Sujet d'une Piece d'Or Millénaire Trouvée à Gao," *Notes Africaines* 60 (1953): 102–03.

18. Insoll, *Islam, Archaeology and History*.

19. See Levtzion and Hopkins, *Corpus*.

20. C. Flight, "Gao 1972: First Interim Report: A Preliminary Investigation of the Cemetery at Sané," *West African Journal of Archaeology* 5 (1975): 81–90; idem, "Gao 1974: Second Interim Report. Excavations in the Cemetery at Sané" (Birmingham [manuscript on file, Centre of West African Studies, University of Birmingham], 1978); idem, "Gao 1978: Third Interim Report: Further Excavations at

Sané" (Birmingham [manuscript on file, Centre of West African Studies, University of Birmingham], 1979).

21. Jean Sauvaget, "Les épitaphes royales de Gao," *Bulletin de l'Institut français de l'Afrique noire* 12 (1950): 418–40; M. M. Vire, "Notes sur trois épitaphes royales de Gao," *Bulletin de l'Institut français de l'Afrique noire, Series B* 20 (1958): 368–76; P. F. de Moraes Farias, "The Oldest Extant Writing in West Africa: Medieval epigraphs from Issuk, Saney, and Egef–n–Tawaqqast (Mali)," *Journal des Africanistes* 60 (1990): 65–113.

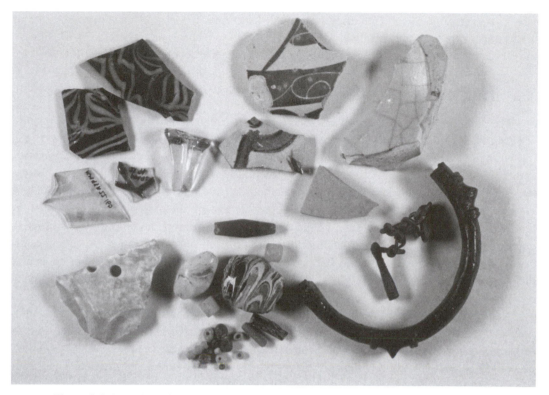

Figure 5.4. Selection of imported trade goods recovered predominantly from Gao Ancien.
Photograph by Timothy Insoll

successively adopting the name of the Prophet and of the first two caliphs, Abu Bakr and Umar.[22]

Neither were stelae confined to Gao-Saney. Gao Ancien was also ringed with Muslim cemeteries, and the inscriptions recovered from these have also provided important information on Islamization processes within the region. At one of the cemeteries, Gorongobo, to the northwest of Gao Ancien, several Muslim tombstones inscribed in Arabic and dating from between 1130 and 1306 were recorded. One tombstone dated to 1210 appears to bear the female Songhai names of either Waybiya or Buwy, depending on the reading. This is of significance as it is first and foremost a Muslim tombstone, bearing a local name, and female as well, and conclusive proof for local conversion to Islam by the early thirteenth century.[23] This further supports the interpretation proposed earlier that we are witnessing indigenous control of trade; trade adapted to suit a local elite, many of whom were Muslim.

This "indigenization" of Islam was also apparent in various other aspects of the archaeological evidence recovered; evidence, moreover, indicating that the impact of Islam was being felt to varying degrees in many aspects of life. The archaeology indicates a picture of complexity, as evident in the internal and intra-site patterning, reflecting the fact that what was being recovered was the residue of both past communities and individuals with varying degrees of adherence to

22. C. Flight, "Thoughts on the Cemetery at Sané" (Birmingham [unpublished paper from the Centre of West African Studies, University of Birmingham], n. d.), p. b:1.

23. P. F. de Moraes Farias, "Appendix 2. The Inscriptions from Gorongobo," in Insoll, *Urbanism*, pp. 156–59.

Islam, or even none at all. Thus this reconstructed picture differs somewhat from the types of broad brush approach adopted historically, which might in passing describe Gao as Muslim by the eleventh century, but in so doing fail to recognize the inherent complexity therein.

ARCHITECTURE

The architecture uncovered, for instance, was representative of these distinctions; a picture of "domestic" Gadei as opposed to "cosmopolitan" Gao Ancien could be reconstructed. In the former, part of a roundhouse built of liquid mud (or banco) was uncovered dating from the eleventh to fourteenth centuries.[24] This type of structure is so far absent in Gao Ancien, where buildings universally employed the right angle and are of fired brick, stone, and mudbrick.[25] Whether the presence of the roundhouse can be associated with the persistence of traditional religion in this quarter is unclear (and unlikely). But such a question can be posited, as in many areas of sub-Saharan Africa there appears to be a correlation between roundhouses and traditional religion, and square or rectangular houses and Islam. Bearing in mind the important caveat that such generalizations inevitably find exceptions to religious explanation, Muslims can live in roundhouses and non-Muslims in architecture employing right angles!

Yet the architecture in Gao Ancien differed considerably, and in style (but not materials), was much more reminiscent of the type of structures encountered at other trade centers in the Western Sahel, such as Tegdaoust and Koumbi Saleh,[26] which were predominantly Muslim. A large mosque with a fired-brick *miḥrāb* was previously recorded within Gao Ancien,[27] while our more recent excavations uncovered part of a palace or rich merchant's house also built of fired brick (fig. 5.5). Elements of a further structure, an aisle, might have been part of another mosque. The remains of a substantial stone-built wall and gatehouse might have once encircled the central citadel, also dating from the twelfth to thirteenth centuries.[28] Such features were lacking in Gadei, again reinforcing this picture of complexity.

PERSONAL POSSESSIONS AND DIET

Within the area of the roundhouse described above, objects with Muslim associations potentially suggest syncretic processes were in operation or that simple architectural correlations and religious types are flawed, as they probably are. For example, a large wooden bead from a set of prayer beads (what is sometimes erroneously referred to as a Muslim "rosary") was recovered from a context dated to between the mid-eleventh and fourteenth centuries.[29] Similarly, and also from Gadei, the remains of what appear to have been an amulet cover were found, a copper casing containing the remains of fibrous matter that might have been the Muslim prayer or invocation contained therein.

24. Insoll, *Urbanism*, pp. 15–17.

25. Insoll, *Islam, Archaeology and History.*

26. Jean Devisse, Abdallah O. Babacar, et al., *Tegdaoust*, Volume 3: *Recherches sur Aoudaghost: Campagnes 1960–1965, enquêtes générales* (Éditions Recherche sur les Civilisations 25; Paris, 1983); Jean Polet, *Tegdaoust*, Volume 4: *Fouille d'un quartier de Tegdaoust (Mauritanie orientale)* (Paris, 1985); Sophie Berthier, *Recherches archéologiques sur la capitale de l'empire de Ghana: Étude d'un secteur d'habitat à Koumbi*

Saleh, Mauritanie: Campagnes II–III–IV–V, (1975/1976–1980/1981) (Cambridge Monographs in African Archaeology 41; British Archaeological Reports, International Series 680; Oxford, 1997).

27. Raymond Mauny, "Notes d'archéologie au sujet de Gao," *Bulletin de l'Institut français d'Afrique noire, Series B* (1951) 13: 837–52.

28. Insoll, *Islam, Archaeology and History*; idem, *Urbanism.*

29. B. Roy, "The Beads," in Insoll, *Urbanism*, p. 106.

Figure 5.5. The palace or rich merchant's house. Photograph by Timothy Insoll

Dietary patterns also differed across and between the sites as represented by aspects of the faunal and botanical remains recovered. A varied picture of resource exploitation was indicated by the faunal remains from Gadei, with both wild and domesticated species present. Of especial interest was the presence of dog remains in contexts dated between the early/mid eleventh and late sixteenth centuries, that is, certainly after Islam was the majority religion in the city. This was interpreted as food refuse owing to the context in which it was found [30] and suggests that a mixed community was resident in Gadei, both Muslim and non-Muslim, or alternatively, Muslims who continued to eat species forbidden under Islamic dietary law.[31] By contrast, dog remains were lacking in Gao Ancien, perhaps to be expected in this evidently more Islamized quarter. Otherwise, the patterns manifest in the species present are broadly comparable to those at Gadei, with both wild and domestic specimens found.

Besides the mammals, fish, shellfish, and birds indicated that a variety of environments were being exploited. Fish and shellfish, though little differentiated between Gao Ancien and Gadei, were obtained from streams, from main channels of the Niger River, pools on the floodplain, fast and slow flowing water, and swampy and reed-filled environments.[32] The picture obtained from the botanical remains recovered from Gadei and Gao Ancien was also broadly similar, samples largely coming from the later occupation levels and providing evidence for rice, dates, local fruits such as the jujube, along with pearl millet, watermelon, and cotton.[33] In terms of connections with Islam, these are indirect, but cotton is generally regarded as an introduction

30. C. Stangroome, "The Faunal Remains from Gadei," in Insoll, *Urbanism*, p. 56.

31. See Insoll, *Archaeology of Islam*.

32. Nicky Milner, "The Marine and Freshwater Molluscs," in Insoll, *Urbanism*, pp. 36–38; H. Cook,

"The Fish Bones from Gadei," in Insoll, *Urbanism*, pp. 38–44.

33. Dorian Q. Fuller, "The Botanical Remains," in Insoll, *Urbanism*, pp. 28–35.

in the Islamic period, that is, after the tenth century,[34] whereas Ziziphus, or jujube stones, are known to have been later used as a raw material in the production of Islamic prayer beads.[35]

Interestingly, on the basis of the cooking equipment found in Gadei and Gao Ancien such as utilitarian pottery, stove fragments, and strainers, MacLean[36] suggests that a "wet" cuisine was preferred in Gao, and that kitchen mobility, a characteristic of Songhai cooking today, was also a factor several hundred years ago.[37] From this evidence it has been possible to reconstruct something of the resultant cuisine, and it appears that many of the bones were subjected to "heavy" chopping, possibly indicating boiling as a cooking method. In other words, this evidence appears to suggest that the maintenance of traditional African cuisine was being upheld, though the diet was largely structured by Islamic law. Again, another indicator of indigenous adaptation of elements of Islamic belief and practice is seemingly apparent in the archaeological record.

SYNCRETISM, TIME, AND IDENTITY

This provides a convenient juncture to return to a brief consideration of the creation and maintenance of Islamic identity both in the Gao region and in its wider context. A key concept that has already been mentioned as of importance here is syncretism. This is the blending or fusing of different religious traditions or elements that can emerge as a practical mechanism for reconciling time, for instance. Although sometimes condemned as a contentious term implying "inauthenticity" or "contamination,"[38] for our purposes in considering religion as change, "syncretism" is preferable to alternatives such as "creolize" or "hybridize."

The need for syncretic process to reconcile time reckoning can take many forms; for example, an agriculturally aligned seasonal system must confront and integrate with a very different religious system.[39] This can occur by conversion to Islam with the imposition of a new calendar, "arranged, without intercalation, to be independent not only of the old Arabian lunar year but especially of all solar reckoning which was traditionally linked to the structures of agricultural society and religion."[40] This does not imply that West African subsistence farmers necessarily used formal calendars, but if agriculture is really a "ritual revealed by the gods or culture heroes,"[41] then the abandonment of associated seasonal, temporal, and ancestral frameworks (the latter possibly key) will be difficult, or alternatively adjustments might be made to allow the continuation of old and new combined.

This would appear to be what occurred with conversion to Islam in the Sahel region of West Africa where it is possible to suggest a model of phased conversion allied with syncretic adaptation based in part on the archaeological data just presented.[42] Within this region the earliest converts to Islam would seem to have been the nomadic populations, precipitated in part through

34. Andrew M. Watson, *Agricultural Innovation in the Early Islamic World: The Diffusion of Crops and Farming Techniques, 700–1100* (Cambridge, 1983).

35. Fuller, "Botanical Remains," p. 30.

36. M. R. MacLean, "The Locally Manufactured Pottery," in Insoll, *Urbanism*, p. 77.

37. M. R. MacLean and Timothy Insoll, "The Social Context of Food Technology in Iron Age Gao, Mali," *World Archaeology* 31 (1999): 78–92.

38. Rosalind Shaw and Charles Stewart, "Introduction: Problematizing Syncretism," in *Syncretism/Anti Syncretism: The Politics of Religious Synthesis*, edited

by Charles Stewart and Rosalind Shaw (London, 1994), p. 1.

39. Insoll, *Archaeology, Ritual, Religion.*

40. F. Denny, "Islamic Ritual: Perspectives and Theories," in *Approaches to Islam in Religious Studies*, edited by Richard C. Martin (Tucson, 1985), p. 71.

41. Mircea Eliade, *The Sacred and the Profane: The Nature of Religion*, translated from the French by Willard R. Trask (New York, 1959), p. 96.

42. Insoll, *Islam, Archaeology and History*; idem, *Urbanism.*

their early exposure to Muslims by acting as their guides in trans-Saharan trade. Equally, the ease with which they converted is not solely explained by notions of familiarity but also, perhaps, through the lesser degree of upheaval involved in nomadic conversion than that suffered by agriculturalists, for instance.[43] Hence factors such as the ease of worship that Islam enjoys would have been significant, allied with a potential by lesser importance ascribed to physical ties to the land, and in turn to the degree of ancestral significance lent to the land as well. In other words, the bonds were more easily broken and syncretic mechanisms reconciling the old and the new were not so essential.

This would certainly seem to be mirrored within the site patterning evident in parts of the Gao region. For example, a map of Muslim cemeteries in the Niger Bend was prepared by de Gironcourt.[44] It is apparent from this map that the majority of the cemeteries containing Muslim inscriptions are to be found clustered along the Niger River, predominantly along the left bank, as well as along the Tilemsi Valley running north from Gao, and to a lesser extent the paleo-tributaries of the Niger River.[45] This cemetery patterning appears to follow the main axes of communication and of trade, that is, those that run through nomad territory,[46] and could indicate both mortality rates among merchants and other Muslim travelers and that nomads were among the first to convert to Islam in this region. As the data presented in the map are "raw" data, a mix of early and more recent material, this must remain a hypothesis.

The second group to convert to Islam within the Western Sahel seems to have been elements of the urban population, and again a practical explanation can be proposed to account for this. Specifically, that they might have benefited from preferable trade conditions with Muslim co-religionists, or alternatively that Islam had an appeal within the urban environment through its ability to provide cohesiveness due to the notion of community (*ummah*) that underpins it. This is a factor of potential significance in overcoming ethnic differences that were perhaps more manifest in towns, settlements with a predilection to throw together a variety of different ethnic, social, and other groups.[47] Such an interpretation would appear to be supported within Gao, however, these urban centers were amorphous forms that attract and release elements of their populations all the time. Their population, theoretically at least, could be forever altering, even if their core remains the same. This means that both within West Africa, and throughout much of sub-Saharan Africa, the ascription "Muslim city" may be tenuous at best. Islamic practice in urban centers such as Gao does not seem to have depended on the development of syncretic mechanisms to reconcile the old with the new, at least it was not quite such a pressing concern in this context, as it was for the third group to be considered, the sedentary agriculturalists.

The last group to convert to Islam in parts of West Africa were the bulk of the population, the sedentary agriculturalists, and within this context the notion of syncretism is vital. This apparent tardiness in conversion may be interpreted as related to conceptual changes described above, that is, the collision of different calendrical and temporal systems which, more than prescribing when crops might be sown or harvested, provided the whole structural framework connected with the lynchpin of African traditional religions, the importance of the ancestors.[48]

---

43. See, for example, Nehemiah Levtzion, "Rural and Urban Islam in West Africa: An Introductory Essay," *Asian and African Studies* 20 (1986): 7–26.

44. Georges R. de Gironcourt, *Missions de Gironcourt en Afrique occidentale, 1908/1909–1911/1912: Documents scientifiques* (Paris, 1920), p. 161.

45. Insoll, *Islam, Archaeology and History*, p. 13.

46. It is unlikely to be unduly influenced by de Gironcourt's survey methodology, as his coverage of the area was very thorough.

47. See Insoll, *Sub-Saharan Africa.*

48. See, for example, John S. Mbiti, *Introduction to African Religion* (London, 1975); Benjamin C. Ray, *African Religions: Symbol, Ritual, and Community* (Englewood Cliffs, 1976).

Ancestral bonds and frameworks linking men to the land were negotiated primarily through structured relationships, "whether with other living people, or with the spirits of the dead, or with animals, or with cleared land, or with the bush."[49] These were beliefs manifest through what Ranger terms "cults," as in the maintenance of cults of the land, for example. The existence of the whole ancestral framework of belief and associated practices meant that conversion to Islam broke with or altered the balance that sustained the conceptual system, as Rene Bravmann[50] argues.

Hence, even though Islam might be well established within the urban environment at centers such as Gao and among nomad groups in the surrounding region, its impact within the remainder of the rural environment was frequently minimal even several hundred years later. This can be indicated archaeologically in various ways, as in the persistence of non-Muslim burial practices, such as the continuation of a tradition of urn burial in a contracted position accompanied by grave goods such as iron bracelets and ankle rings[51] found at the site of Toguere Doupwil in the Inland Niger River Delta area of Mali, farther west along the Niger River. This was evidence dated to the fifteenth century, and thus long after conversion to Islam had occurred in urban centers such as Timbuktu, which is closer to the Inland Niger River Delta than Gao. Similarly, the continuation of production of anthropomorphic and figural terra-cotta statuettes, contrary to Islamic proscription on the replication of figurative imagery, is found up to and even beyond a similar date. At the urban center of Jenne-jeno, for example, also in the same region of Mali, over seventy animal or human representations have been recovered; the function is interpreted in various ways, including for protection, and in "ancestor worship."[52] However, these interpretations are based upon ethnography, oral tradition, and parallels with material from elsewhere in the region.

Where conversion did take place, syncretism of Islamic and traditional religions frequently occurred, seemingly as a mechanism for reconciling issues such as the collision of frameworks of time and their associated implications for conceptions of land, its links with people and ancestors, issues of possession, fertility, and the like. Although relevant archaeological data are still sparse for the Western Sahel from the fourteenth century onwards, large-scale conversion amongst sedentary agriculturists seems to have been limited until more recently. In some instances it occurred only after the collapse of the great states such as Songhai. As Levtzion notes,[53] when the great states disappeared and the urban foundation of the religion crumbled in the seventeenth and eighteenth centuries, this meant that Muslims moved into the countryside, "and won adherents among peasants and fishermen, who had hardly been influenced by Islam before."

Again if we consider the Gao region, though it has to be acknowledged that the data are sparse, these general interpretations are ostensibly supported. Various settlements south of Gao, for example, sent various commodities up the Niger River, the most important of which was gold obtained from the Sirba Valley in Niger.[54] Close to this place an Islamic "frontier" appears

49. T. O. Ranger, "African Traditional Religions," in *The Study of Religion, Traditional and New Religions*, edited by Stewart Sutherland and Peter Clarke (London, 1991), p. 109.

50. René A. Bravmann, *Islam and Tribal Art in West Africa* (African Studies Series 11; Cambridge, 1974).

51. Rogier Bedaux, "Mali," *Nyame Akuma* 8 (1976): 41.

52. R. J. McIntosh and S. K. McIntosh, "Terracotta Statuettes from Mali," *African Arts* 12/2 (1979): 52.

53. Nehemiah Levtzion, "Rural and Urban Islam in West Africa: An Introductory Essay," *Asian and African Studies* 20 (1986): 15.

54. See Jean Devisse, "L'Or," in *Vallées du Niger*, edited by Jean Devisse (Paris, 1993), pp. 344–57.

to have existed,[55] indicated by sites such as Bentiya (Kukiya) and Egef-N-Tawaqqast, sites where Arabic funerary inscriptions dating from the thirteenth to fifteenth centuries have also been recorded.[56] Evidence for Islam dating from before the fifteenth century is lacking farther south of this point, both direct, such as mosques and burials, and indirect, such as trade goods sourced from the Muslim World.[57] Even close to Gao, an early center of Islam with its mosques, Muslim burials, even rectangular architecture, survey evidence[58] is rare or late in date, excluding that interpreted as nomad associated, as already described. This is a pattern that appears to be repeated elsewhere in the region, but the overall absence of archaeological research outside of the main urban centers limits what can be inferred from this sort of evidence.

CONCLUSIONS

Although hampered by a lack of archaeological research in general in the Western Sahel (and throughout West Africa), and certainly outside the major historical urban centers such as Gao and Timbuktu, archaeological patterning of some social interest can be seen. The complexity redefines organization of urban composition and trade for acceptance of and adherence to Islam, and the impact of Islam upon social identity.

Conversion to Islam by the inhabitants of Gao occurs, and in a far from uniform process, and is structured by socio-economic affiliation, whether nomads, city-dwellers, or sedentary agriculturalists. Equally this did not entail a whole-scale abandonment of older traditions or traditional religions, as with the tardiness evident in Islamic conversion amongst the sedentary agriculturalists; likewise social aspects such as continuing adherence to traditional cuisines and diets, as might be expected. The latter is more unexpected in having greater fundamental implications in terms of breaking, rather than merely stretching, Islamic religious requirements.

This should certainly not come as a surprise. Throughout sub-Saharan Africa the agency of syncretism has been adopted as a mechanism to reconcile Islam with older traditions in an ongoing process of reconstructing social and religious identities. We as archaeologists are privileged to be able to gain an insight into such processes at work and thus should strive to maximize both recovery and interpretation from the rich archaeological record that Islamic sites frequently yield. In so doing we can more fully assess the notion of changing social identities across the geographical diversity that is the Islamic world.

55. John O. Hunwick, *Shari'a in Songhay: The Replies of al-Maghīlī to the Questions of Askia al-Ḥājj Muḥammad* (London, 1985).

56. Farias, "Oldest Extant Writing," pp. 105–06; N. Arazi, "An Archaeological Survey in the Songhay Heartland of Mali," *Nyame Akuma* 52 (1999): 38–39.

57. Insoll, *Sub-Saharan Africa*.

58. S. Dawa, "Inventaire des sites archéologiques dans le cercle de Gao: Mémoire de fin d'études." (Ph.D. diss., École Normale Supérieure de Bamako, 1985); Insoll, *Islam, Archaeology and History*, pp. 11–15; Arazi, "Archaeological Survey," p. 36.